Copyright © 2023 by Emőke B'Rácz

All rights reserved.

Published in the United States by Leaning Chair Press,
a division of Malaprop's Bookstore/Cafe
ISBN 978-0-9658657-4-6

B'Rácz, Emőke
Hopscotch on the riverbank, while waiting.../ Emőke B'Rácz

1. Poetry

Printed in the United States of America on acid-free paper

First Edition 2023

LEANING
CHAIR
PRESS

www.malaprops.com/leaningchair

Book design by Robert Bradley

Hopscotch on the riverbank, while waiting...

Emőke B'Rácz

LEANING
CHAIR
PRESS

Dedicated to

Grandmothers Time and Wisdom.

Zsofia and Ilona

Special thanks to my Editor Kip Pettersen

and My Wonderful AMANUENSIS

Beverly Reicks

in Florence, Italy

My Family

near and far

and

Gail Addis MLP

"…But remember, make an effort to remember or, failing that, invent."

Monique Wittig

Hopscotch on the riverbank, while waiting…

Emőke B'Rácz

Self

After all, I can't help but be myself…

the clock on the wall went tic toc toc
i skidded along to rhythms outside of myself
for what is expected at fifty-eight years
has knocked on my door
loudly, madness encroaching
you were not there
the sky bound by a double rainbow screaming
yes, yes…there is a…something unnamed
for it can not be uttered out
      loud 'til the end of all times
when faith and every breath
      is on a time in your head
…and it is going off…the alarm.

come and be within the cauldron of your soul
be a patient of your past and your
futuristic life that no one
on this planet could imagine…why write your memoirs
it will be all ashes and anyway the winds
scatter the rumor I called my life…and better yet
i must know the truth
i call myself

to know is to end
to seek is to find
to share is to strengthen
to cry is to wash off the sand
to torture and pry myself
off the comfort of this veiled un reality
to be a love and still hold
shadow shattering dreams.

Brown hair,
brown eyes
pear shaped body
once fluid and sprite
remembers herself
in this body fully planted
at age 57 and a half.

Damn immigrant

The dream woke me with laughter in my heart.

I was in a predicament,
not clear as to if it was my own doing or not
but I found myself
(and this interests me that I choose I found myself instead of anything else)
in a class that was Latin 401. Not Latin 101, but Latin 401.
The students, me amongst them dumbfounded, were conversing in Latin.
I was musing over the situation and I could hear myself thinking
"Well, if you could learn English, you can learn Latin easy."
An overachiever even in my dreams,
oh yeah, the immigrant.

April

APRIL   SUNDAY

    APRIL

SUN MAKES

GOLDEN FRINGES

ON THE RIM OF MY HAT

UNDER   WHICH

CONTINUOUSLY

I HIDE.

The Box maker   October 21, 2004

The paper is white
The scissors are ready surrounded by colors
Like a surgeon
I cut the paper out
All that I do not want
And All that is not for me
Healing into
a sacred space

I take the edge and hold it to the light
To allow what is given
To enter me, to enter the box
It is a small thing in life.
But holding it gives me a smile
I made that and
Putting in on the shelf near by
I glance back
And know what is inside the box and

What I gave to myself to remember
To kindle the spirits
To have a secret place
For secret words and thoughts
To inspire
To keep the hand scribing
Inside and out…in search of
The next poem and the next.

To write is to breathe into the box
The universe that i holds
The universe that surrounds it
It all matters
And matters not to any one
But the journey I am on.

Box maker   2

I made a box out of paper in class.
Now the craze has taken over, child and all
Cannot eat a meal without
folding another box. Everyone
is occupied with creating their own.

Will we get buried in making boxes
your box, the coffin
the funeral pyre, will you be holding your creation
the box, tied in your hands
over your chest
forgotten is the prayer wheel,
the upturned palms
the offering of yourself
to God,
a box is to catch the first fire.

To change the world, begin your box.

April 16, 1993

The sun plays hopscotch on my back
my fingers ice skate on the keyboard
where the cold and the heat meets
my heart lives

I am not sure if I love you or the land you are of
the air I crave, the smells, the passion
time will separate us and our feelings,
she is good at that.
the music will always be there

April 9

The pink blossoms in the front yard are in full bloom
the dogwoods reached their white just as we reached
love's door to heaven.
The Chinese music lulled my soul to peace.
You come to rescue me.

April 14

The poet from Ireland, clad in dark blue,
sat to the side while Mary Margaret,
in college fervor, mouthed her opening statement.
I watched the poet, calm and reticent,
rise and walk to the podium,
her left eyelid lazy and her mouth like her
homeland, round and aching with sadness.
I came to listen to your words,
to rest at your shore.

July 8

It is a morning of sweet dampness.
Summer is sleeping late.
I am sitting while the coffee is brewing,
waiting as I wait all my life.
Waiting has the stigma attached. It is indecisive,
they say,
      for those who do not know what they want,
they say,
        like the time for an appointment,
        inactivate, fruitless,
they say,
      time wasted
they say.
They say many things about many things.
I am waiting for life to unfold.

Folk songs I remember from my childhood

One

With breast full of songs
the song bird lands in the wheatfield
in the skies she already cried her heart out
among the wheatflower in their shadow
the song bird thinks back to her first true love.

Two

The first wind of Spring
to flower a flower
every bird chooses a mate
to flower a flower

I wonder who I should choose
to flower a flower
you choose me and I choose you
to flower a flower.

Three

There are 13 ruffles to my skirt
I think I will marry this summer
but I see it won't come to much
12 of those ruffles will have to be given up.

Patterson

Fredrick sat cross-legged, chanting
idonotwantchildren, idonotwantchildren
I   do   not   want   children
in my amazement at the pounding words
I bowed my head silently under the
storm.
He wrote a year later and said, just as
well,
he found a man and could love him
without
the threat of children. 20 years later and
childless
I recall his words, and I am glad, we are
who we are, childless.
Moments before menopause I chant
those words, affirming
for myself that a child of mine would be
lost and beaten by this world.
I would not be here to stand up and
clean the air, to fight for food and I
still do not understand how people do
not hold back and create more
children. You would have been a great
mother - friends say and I look at
them and say I am a good mother aren't
I, and smile at them.
I do not know about a good wife, though
- my mother interjects
probably not, I agreed with her on the
phone.
You like your life and that's good.
We hang up and I watch the shadows
lifting over my head, was that an
approval from my mother I wondered
and went to bed.
I am harsh on my mother.
I love her ocean deep.

Manmade

I catch myself in the overhead mirrors
at the grocery stores
a middle-aged, white woman
pastey, frozen
movement
lacking
inert.

In a manmade world
all items, ads, goods
everything is
manmademanmade.

Slowness surrounds me
kids breeze by my cart
the thawing
brings me back.

Yes,
it was my choice
not to make
another
manmade artifact.

What is buried underground

or

She had forgiven me, it was me who had not forgiven myself
(Tennessee Williams in a letter to Tallulah Bankhead)

SHE HAD FORGIVEN ME

The echo still strikes against metal, a harsh sliding screeching intrusion on the soul. The betrayal she does not see, blinded by her own infernal engine…screeching, coming to a halt like the 5 o'clock freight train at the depot…back and forth…feelings…sitting in the car, waiting, back and forth, waiting to see which way the train goes, left to forgive…..right not to…is it that simple…the echo still strikes the chords in this cold, doomed, cathedral ceiling inside my flesh.

SHE HAD FORGIVEN ME

…does that mean all is better now?
…does that mean all is forgiven?
…Now i am an ok person again?
…What have i committed?
This feels like the times i look in the mirror and in those moments of loneliness i do not see myself, i only see what is behind me…what is that a picture of? The moments take refuge in the glass, not giving anything back. Imagine Friday morning, and it is not the 13th, between 7 and 8 a.m. and all the mirrors took refuge in the glass. Would the president even stop for a moment or is that a natural no-reflection on him, so it would go unnoticed. How about the inmates in the cells thumping the bibles seeing, i mean not seeing their own reflections. Could that, would that moment be enough of a respite for Mother Nature to recollect and revive without our humane-ly management?

SHE HAD FORGIVEN ME

What if i had committed a horrible act against her person? Am i not responsible for that act? What she does with her forgiveness is her business. I have only myself. I felt betrayed. I feel trapped between the mirror and her forgiveness. Smashing comes to mind.

IT WAS ME WHO HAD NOT FORGIVEN MYSELF

i am tall and beautiful and never has the drudgery of life intruded on my mind. i keep it all in the attic where only i am allowed to enter. It is my world and you are not welcome to it. So many ask, how do you keep your beauty and such good cheer about you?…and is say to them…i never ask for forgiveness because i live in the attic and nobody intrudes there, not even myself…nothing to forgive me for. i never forgive myself.

IT WAS ME WHO HAD NOT FORGIVEN MYSELF

i leev in ton, an Carolina Alley fo many yers now. i had a son, gave him up, jacob was the name i have never given him, befor a white lady took it and gave me 100 dollar for him. i sing to him every night now for 20 yers, he be fine without me for a mamma. i look through bottles and see his face clearly, though i never laid eyes on him now for 20 yers, he be fine without me for a mamma.

IT WAS ME WHO HAD NOT FORGIVEN MYSELF

i take my friends to heart. i do not expect betrayal to be part of friendship. Friendship always felt somehow sacred to me. i always feel that i am responsible even for how others react in that friendship. Now i know otherwise but the pain and the shadow is slow to fade. It is alive and goes through all the degrees of the spectrum as we hold this friendship between us. Without the falling out, how do i know its strength and value. Nothing comes without pain…The pain in my chest as i remember, as i breathe is constant. i am alive and feel a monstrous presence.

SHE HAD FORGIVEN ME

The letter was handwritten and long to figure out. She felt i did not do right by her lover. She kept repeating in the letter that i hurt her lover's feelings by who i am and how i saw their relationship and by the mere fact that i loved my friend more than her new lover. The letter was handwritten, spiked, neatly titled letters harbored such cruel words that intended to hurt and they did do that…can one stop loving a friend because she has a new lover. Must she feel hurt by who i am and that i love her more, as i always will. can she forgive me, ever? She says she has forgiven me but then again they broke up two years after i received that letter.

IT WAS ME WHO HAD NOT FORGIVEN MYSELF

The dream started in Alaska. The houses were close to each other like young animals huddling for body heat. In the dream i kept saying again and again…with an incredulous heart…my sister, she even came to visit me in faraway Alaska…unbelievable…When i awoke i knew that my psyche sister was reassuring me that my sister has not abandoned me for her husband. Is blood not thicker than sex? Can a person so dear in my heart escape my request for remembering who i am in her life and who she is in mine. Why Do i ask for so much?

SHE HAS FORGIVEN ME

Grandmother asked me for my towel to dry herself with and i said NO. i even elaborated that i did not want her old body touching my towel. She looked at me with eyes that i will never forget. What has given me such fear of old age at such young age? I was not bombarded with barbie doll ads (sounds like a nazi subplot) and Clairol commercials at that point of my life yet already i had fear of death, actually i meant to say fear of wrinkled flesh. This happened almost 35 years ago and there are days when i get a whiff of that memory as i lift the towel to my face.

IT WAS ME WHO HAD NOT FORGIVEN HERSELF

my nephew was 6 when i was ten. It happened over new year's eve when the family gathered for good cheer and company. We had a great day running wild in the hills behind our house. Our parents stayed close to the house so we had the whole hillside to ourselves. The snow was knee-deep and our sled had shiny edges with so many runs it almost whistled just standing still. The hot chocolate grandmother made was the best, ever, in my life that night. Andrew was allowed to stay overnight, we were inseparable that day of our life. By nine o'clock we had so much running around we begged for the bed. He and i shared my bed. I never had a boy in my bed before, i knew something was different and never would be the same. We read and snuggled up to each other like two esses. Show me yours he said and i almost did not know what he meant but he was whispering and i knew what he meant. finally i said ok but i made him promise he would let me teach him how to ride the bicycle some day…what a deal we agreed with a glad heart. Hesitantly i searched the comforter for the unfamiliar. My hand curved and gently grasped his willie. What strangeness. Just a touch of my hand and his eyes closed tight, crooning softly…yes, that's it. His hand felt furtive but warm deep down there and i was feeling hot around my ears which never seemed to fade even after he fell asleep and i was left alone in my confusion. He still writes to me and speaks around that night, wishing we were back then. He does not like his life, his wife and his son irritate him and he mistreats his family just like his own father had. He has never forgiven me for leaving his continent.

SHE HAD FORGIVEN ME
Matilda was my classmate and friend. We had the same piano teacher. My family did not have a piano so i practiced over at her house. She remains in my memory like a deer, brown eyes and hair and a slender soul. We had decided to try out what this kissing business was all about. I remember the day so clearly because of the priest. I was on my way home and she was standing inside the fence. We reached and clasped our hand on top of each others tightening our hold over the wrought iron flower. The pattern deeply etched in my memory as we leaned in to touch our lips…just at that moment the local priest was strutting by, witnessing our innocence. His fingers flew up in a threatening stance as he pulled us apart and sent us to hell. Sins of the flesh, he said and sent me on my way to home. I ran and ran until i could not breathe any longer. His towering figure turned left and i felt forever chased by this cloaked man. Matilda, I heard, died in prison three years ago. The details are not clear as to the reason for her early departure. Part of my heart went with her. Part of her lives within me.

Selves

To Carolyn Forché

The mountains have asked for your presence
the rivers go out of their banks to draw you in
I sing songs of enchantment
will you come sing your words
will you come and sooth my soul
will you come share your fire

The words will push you out of the cradle
the son you bore keeps you sane
the songs you write keep you dreaming.

Swan song

I remember how she moved
her shadow thrown against the wall
her hair flew, at the movement of her head
like a swan
hunted down, last gasp.

By the meditation garden

Some one just walked by
a car drove by
Norma sits next to me on the bench, pressing time.

The drummer walks by, all clad in white.
Moved smoothly at Tai Chi this morning, I noticed
his movements like
notes on a music sheet, all connected
I was surprised at such force in a state of gracefulness.
He walks by again playing with his bead necklaces, such dexterity, gentleness
such force he calls forth from his drum
I stand and watch in awe of this man.

I never could guess what he would do next, throw
his necklaces with impatience onto the grass
or continue with the cat's cradle
not with anger but without care, he is capable of that
detached
is what disturbs me about this man.
To be detached instantaneously, when the drumming stops
when and how we learn to do that.

Suddenly I realize the answer to all that, yep it is money
Time is money
life is money
emotions are costly, because they take away time
from making money
Yes, the founder of the
Bank of Emotional Investment

NORMA(L)

They called her Normal at age six, she recalls for her therapist.
She hated it.
Her older sister was Creative
Beautiful
Her unborn brother is surely going to be Talented
Handsome
To be normal is all she knew of herself,
and she never knew to be anything else.
Normal, a flat word
no edges, no laughter, no anger.
Normal is unlike the circus,
the dancer, the painter.
The N being cold, angular set off by O that opposed such existence.
The M that towered and spread taking up space, just like a man,
constricts the R from becoming red hot like a Latin lover.
The A pricking her excellence only to be defused by L in the end.

In South Carolina

She can't believe how drunk she is.
She is trying to be normal, to sound like herself.
Void crashes through her like a freight train
at the crossing
unexpectedly, it came out of nowhere, from the left.
She sat at the crossing, trying to focus and gain some strength.
She feels drained, removed from life.
The train that stole her heart is afar.

It is six a.m.
She does not belong to anyone anywhere
so she sits at the crossing.
There is no car behind her to nudge her into action
so she sits there.

Grayness enfolds her inside
while ally fog rules over the outer edge.
She drank too much last night, that's a fact.
Normal is approaching her in a red pickup truck and fast.

Normal, who needs it!
She heads North.
She forgets her name.

Collaboration

In the picture her eyes have told the story of the world
they anchored me to my destiny
how she knew that I needed to see her eyes
how she knew to speak wisdom for breakfast each morning
is beyond me.

My eyes are dark brown
like a barrel full of rain water
eyes like holes that bleed the world into them
eyes that speak in sorrow
eyes that hold thunder and lightning
For each drop of rain
a faint smile passes through her eyes.
The flowers of the meadow reflect in them.
The aroma of an august sunset
holding echoes
sounding the trumpets
eyes that hold tight
as if the ocean is your mother.
Hold tight as if forever has just passed through the iris
into the stronghold of the mind,
much of it in shadow.

Emöke B'Rácz, Betty Holden, Lish Morphew, Zoe Rhine

At rest

with pleasing aches of hardworked days

in your thighs and thoughts.

You depart from them

like wild geese for warmer parts

to return in future

thoughts refined.

Camomile tea for the body

and what is for the mind ?

dream with me
              of fields of
              tulips
              poppy flowers
dance with me
              and happy children
              old and young
smile with me
              and sing songs
              to our steps

              are you with me?

Dreaming

Sunday tea dance in the school gym
grandmothers in one corner, chaperoning
like sparrows on the wire, the girls chattering
the boys like nervous animals, caged, across the room.

The warmth of women's company electrified my dream.
The choice was there for cocksucking
or an embrace…
falling onto yearning lips I made the choice
again and again.

Like the axle holding the wheels
so strongly held the desire.
I became the axle, swiftly flying above roads.
The struggle was long to become the driver, to gain direction.

Went to buy a car, stole the prototype
ran down unfamiliar streets without fear
clutching this manmade monster to my breasts
with a final heave I threw it
for destruction it headed.
The weight lifted.
I returned for a quiet chinese meal with a womanfriend.

We walked the streets freed.
The evening welcomed our footsteps.
The city. (softened)
(it) seem like homecoming.

Dreaming 2

the dream was filled with poets,
Carolyn Forché and her students.
I was taken ill so I was not in her class
but outside, laying down.
my uncle walked by looking for her.
He was looking to find out the name of one of her students,
a young man, he suspected he was a spy.
I did not feel the intrigue,
I just wanted to get my letter to the teacher.
my lungs felt heavy,
like a tons of bricks on me, without pain.

Dreaming 3

the room's four corners look the same

but every time i look at one

there is a different shadow living in memory's web

who can tell

the child sees not.

Eating a candy

From the corner of your eye
you spot the wrap in your purse

or your fingers find the familiar
shape without looking

or
your mouth wants the sweetness
and you begin the search for it

or
someone holds out in their hand
round, gold wrapped, inviting.

you know it is time for candy.
the unwrapping takes no time at all
the hand reaching the mouth
takes no time at all

the lips are perched for the contact
the tongue already budding its nodes
the saliva readily gathering
and you swallow to make room
for candy

it could happen anywhere
in bed after making love
driving home in a rain storm
or four in the morning
when sleep avoids you body
or at work there is an unconscious knowing
that it is time for candy

the messenger goes and brings the reward
hands a handful over
behind the register
we all line up for a treat

smooth, caramel coffee taffy
gooey

The candy and its sweetness
or sourness or nutty chocolate center

it is there
you know what you are getting
and the moment is named
just that eating candy.

Etherized

Men intrude with their eyes
at the domes of my soul.
The surgeon said-make that four hours, nurse
and I gasped the ether, deeper.

The floating sensation began.
I was flying above cities and land
an eden, untouched, unspoiled.
The oven cradled icebergs
the air, frozen, cut like a knife
the sun dipped in the west
for just tonight escaping the red clouds
uncapped, wakened
I drew my hands
until I touched
the illusion of two swollen breasts.

The fire

When the body was added
I heard the screaming swallowed by the fire.
My bones still echo it.

The marrow
remembers everything.
It haunts the joints.
It squeezes the last breath out of me
as it falls on the floor.
It shatters.
It reflects
one thousand times
for you to see
that once the body is added
the lines softly go supine.

For your son

With such joy in your eyes
you follow his movements
your fingers lost in the air
as you speak your words
yes, you created him too.
You gave him firm feet
ensurance of soul
now you are giving him your words
the road map.

Found echoes

The forest is within her sight
the meadow holds her hostage.
A cantor, she sings in circles
her hymns rise in a straight line.

She has no desire
no determination to go anywhere.
She is wandering

the field open to her
entangling grass to sky.

She is nowhere in the everywhere.

The echo
the originator into oneness
of millions of stars.

How can she not go into madness
the comforter
the choice.

The evening collapses
the dreams sprout through her eyes
her mouth
deafens the thunders.

She prays
as she climbs the lightning's zig-zag
She is everywoman.
What is it to touch down on the wild side
of herself, who lives there
what grows well?

Old woman
her failing hands
hair reaching the sky

words unattached from her mouth

She walks as she prays
repeating
re-inventing the chaos
she lives on the outside of her dreams.

Mathematical symbols chart in the Chambers 20th Century Dictionary

plus or minus is equal to or maybe is not equal to
but far greater than, is not greater than, it is less than one equal to
at the intersection, union is a member of the set, as subset of difference
denotes an operation
implying an empty set
maps into because the angle parallel
perpendicular to the factorial x, varies directly as infinity
imaginary square root of minus one
imaginary cube root of one
the ratio of the circumference
the circle to its diameter approximates the base of natural logarithms
the eccentricity of a conic sections, common logarithm
to base n, Naperian approaches the limit a.
The sum of terms indicated absolutely the mean value of x.
The differential coefficient of y with respect to x
is integral.

3 panels, contemporary window
old white
the shadow of the windowframe
warmgray
the glass or its presence
is
of no importance
the life in between the breasts
oldwhite and warmgray is full.
The electric hum vibrates
paleblue
without being present.
Life below the windows is calm and eternal.
The depth, the distance
grows each moment
the opportunity to travel, to learn
is infinite.
The source of light is omnipotent
in its simplicity
is everything.

3 stars came crashing through the spider's web.
2 stars with only four points,
did not escape her netting.
The web was studded with fuschia triangles.
Her memories sat on 5 drops of sky
as she looked at a picture with 14 little girls in it,
each holding ice cream cones, vanilla is her guess,
except the little girl on the left
who cradles a blue toy soldier on her lap.
In her smile was the faint memory
of a wish that never came true.

Create

Consider this day.
Cats walk on your grave.
Open and closed.

Three pens on my desk.
Yellow ants in a blue box.
The writing always begins there.

Palenque, Mexico

I am sitting in the sun
unmoving
except my arm, writing.
Sweat beads upon my upper lip.
The shadow animals are dancing on the paper.
I am writing within these shadows.
The words are genetically struggling
to get outside their own limits.
My other hand holds a half-eaten cracker in mid-air
unmoving.
The sun beats upon the right side of my face.
The birds on my left, call evening to ascend.
The birds on my right, like crazed souls, caught.
The jungle has many faces.
My shoulders are exposed,
a textile knot fills the space between my breasts.
My eyes are filled with dancing words.
The breasts complete the fruit pattern in the cloth,
sunsensuous
unmoving
Carved steps lead me to the waterfall.
I immerse in the ancient.

Advice to young writers

Many a time I get to read
Writing from young people
Who think I am the cat's pyjamas
Looking for encouragement

I read their work and sigh
Some have potential others need not
Continue but for themselves
I feel the frustration and want to yell

Go live a life before you write about it
The imagination is not enough
To express a life on paper.
It is a good exercise for just that.

To be a writer I need to tell them
Is to live a life worth writing about
To connect and create new passages
The life has to be matured

The writing lies flat on the paper without
The breath of sweet heartbreak
The writing lies flat on the paper
Without a life lived

Go work washing dishes
Sweeping the streets, experiencing
The elements of nature
Observe form your own heart

The world at large is large
Live and be
The writer will show up then.
You can count on yourself turning blue

The writer in you
will turn blue without telling the truth.

Dancing is good for the Soul

Sunday dusk find us
four women around a square table,
the dance begins.

One take a moment out from writing, to slurp her coffee
The other leans back on her chair
The third on places her left hand on the paper
as if to hold the floor, for dancing, steady.

The legs have their place too.
The blue chested adverb stretches one leg,
the other leg rests at an angle on the rung of the chair
the fourth moves backward, as her pen stops in mid-air
with the index finger tapping.
It is within this circle that we attract the words
asking for a dance.

Picasso's Gertrude Stein

lines
intensely amberstruck
she learns
ready for the truth of it
wordstruck
explosion

in flight
How has it fallen up?

The neck supports a world of questions
in midflight
the stars are brightest
the clouds she sends
whirling word dust
the rocks go through me
as she leans in to my face
she impels words
sweet ecstasy.

Angels of MJ Kirby-Smith

The angels came with plasterdust sitting
in the bends of the flesh
a vegetable of heavenly mischief.

the green to brackish black
dazzled, molded into permanence
your vision
entrapped
a flow of captured moments
your sculpture
entrapped
my words pressed to
white pages
entrapped

the Redneck Angel
Angel doing Handstand
and the
Young Angel with Faded Hightop
sit in Malaprop's windows
collecting moments, never aging or fading
dusty but only skin deep
angels will outlast children
your creations, too.

Domino, Dominus, Domini

Words around my tongue, I feel
them rising, diving for depths
I do not have the wisdom to know.
On my tongue perches a little thought,
full of words as to the reason
I'm deaf and dumb.
I live with the nuns at St. Elizabeth's,
toward the cross
I turn and toss in my bed
as words bombard my walls,
tightly, my lips press to the whiteness
licking words off, swallowing them.

My lips twist and turn my face
grotesque. The nuns come
watch until dawn.
The pearls drop, collect in a silver bowl
my words, the offering
each night after midnight mass
waiting for the sun to reach the fifth column
my lips, eyelids
they shimmer to wakefulness.
I gasp as all words leave my body
parched, wordless.
I adore wordless days. I see,
I listen and savor the smells
all taken in to memory.
Spendthrift night, the mistress
will free my lips to whisper, to tenderly suck air
between moments of indecision.
I like the silence my lips capture and afford me
after words have been spoken.
There is a gate, always flooded
by scrupulous words.

Words endlessly emigrate to new lands
filling their own shapes, forcing our lips
landscaping our minds.

There are no monsters under my bed, I reassure myself
each night before I ask the light to go silent
I pray to the dream queen for another story
to fill the cold pages with bodies twisted in fright
by night we sail and tell stories to others and fill their pillow cases
with creatures small and large, cold and hot bodies
sweating and twisting with another story needing to be dreamt.

The case of the butterfly that consumes children for lunch
the dragon that always chases us to the wall where the scream
always silently brings the dreamer back to their room
in cold sweat.

The whole in the sidewalk matched the whole in the sky
in waiting it lies for tipped up souls to swallow
the cement is as hard as the clouds are permeable
the sighs of man and beast follow the cries of birds
in early morning as life shatters into day.

Hot coffee in mug awaiting my lips
the smoke enters the lungs, again and again
the desire to live is weak and fragile
the love this body harbors is greater than the sky but all is
not adding up to the mind and its torturous journey.

To write, and to write some more
who is to listen and who is to write
and if it is written
the reader will yawn and cough up
phlegm to clear the passage.

Words enter into us daily
unlike medicine, we heed not the power
it exercises, the words
burrow under our skin
into our minds
leaving the heart floundering.

So many words from so many hearts
go unheeded or it feel like it
the power is used up and we are desensitized
to borrow without a reprieve
to cruelty without end
so how is the heart
how are the words to remain
what is
and what is not
grounds for breaking the soil for spring gardening.

I ready book for clues in my life
I search corners of my room for memories
to find the thread that connects
you and me and the stars and the river and the baby goat

is it not miraculous that we are all here
at the same moment breathing
dreaming our lives
unread pages entice me to keep searching
and when I get a glimpse of myself
I run and busy the hand again with
chores that fill the gap of the intake and
the moment you breathe out again
there I am lost and frozen in time
how shall the inborn act of wanting
create the next moment
the mystery is always there but I forgot to look
and sigh the sigh of relief that life in spite of myself
chooses to go grow and fill out with you
in it and brightly pointing to a goal and the next
moment there I am again wanting to suck in air

and blowing it out again
The blue of inertia dances in front of my eyes
we hold our breath, us women
longer than any other creature I can imagine
refusing such in born talent
to breath in and out
again the stars are visible in that moment of blue
and the body says go on take it in
all of it

mango juice is from the fruit that goddess favored
I imagine

empty page
empty page
sex addicts on TV
sex addicts on streets
sex addicts in daytime
at night the need is

empty page
empty page
drugs flowing into veins
the children wish to better the world
by destroying themselves

empty page
empty page
the driver buckles her belt
a drunken man still
destroys

empty page
empty page
how do I sing songs
how do I praise thee

empty page
empty page
like this, my child
like this.

Personal/Politics

After Pineapple Merwin

do you know who invented war
do you know why war was invented
do you know who killed first, beast or man
do you know why men like to fight
do you know why we eat dead flesh
do you know?

do you know
we are killing each day and night, ourselves
do you know you cannot kill without killing yourself
do you know how very good we are at this
do you know that men don't care to cry
do you know why the killing starts
at the hearth and in the holy houses

do you have the money to buy a gun
do you want to go and fight, shoot one off
do you know why you are with your lover
do you know if birds sleep at night or

do you care or should you
do you know you are the best enemy
do you know you will fight yourself your whole damn life
do you know why you need enemies to stay alive
do you know a nursery rhyme, every word
do you know why we need nuclear arms
why is green the color of hope

do you know why eyes are not violet or orange
do you know what is in your genes and what they are and
do you know that you have choices
or do you?

The authors are reading

Welcome to the Warren Wilson sitcom show
Silver and Wachtel
give us gas to forget
the newsreel
from Yugoslavia where
a different breed of men
just began
to kill one another
we are still not sure of the outcome
and why it started!

The bee-keeper

The land you are of is under siege
the women are with madness
they hover and dance
like bees outside the hive
disturbed by the smoke and shouts.

They wait to establish their roots again
the hive moved
and no one knows where the bee-keeper has gone.

You send a letter, a direction indicated
each night I fly and find you
comforting both of us in this madness
embraced, upon the road without words
I find life tasteless.

Favorite myth from my childhood

King Mattyas went around the country disguising himself as a migrant worker. He worked among the men and in special ways marked what he had worked on. He ate the meager food that was given to the day laborers. He shared housing, the cold the heat and the physical pain of hard work. After a job was done he returned to his castle and put on the royal clothing. Shortly he would return to the feudal lord whose lands he worked. The feudal lord would not recognize him as a laborer on his property because he never paid attention to the fate of the laborers. The King would begin a conversation about the laborers and ask about the treatment they received while employed by the lord. This is when he would reveal who he was and prove that he worked there by making the lord see his markings. The proof was there, plain to see. King Matthyas would always teach the lord a lesson, a lesson that would last a lifetime. He was always just and for the people. By the end of the story I would cheer and whoop around my room for justice was served.
King Matthias was famous for being on the side of the common soul. He also valued literature and the arts. His famous library was Korvina Press which was burned in the 1500s by the Ottomans. His symbol was the Raven.

come
put your hands on my shoulder
this world is cold
outsiders passing
looking into nothingness
shaking the tree in the wrong season
no fruits will hit the ground

come
turn to the drifters
helping hands hold you up
it is all so dark
stars of charcoal
gleaming in the blue sky
shimmering bodies
loneliness by self denial
friends turning from you
no one can be one with you
nothing ever meets.

Aimless

the wanderer comes asks for bread
has not seen his child awhile
all things that are free in life
has not seen his child awhile

poised an empty church
no folks to warm the inside
they have not seen god awhile
no folks to warm the inside

by the time he greets the sea
the sun is down
only the northern wind reddening
from within the setting sky

has not see his child awhile
has not felt god inside
aimless
the wanderer comes and asks for bread.

An American Sport

She is 69 years old,
still bowls to stay young
and to impress her husband.
Strike, strike, strike…I am hot!
Look at me, honey, she says
I can throw this ball right through the pins
with such bounce.
that the alley fills with my echoes…
yeah, yeah he says
…and you still think it's nothing!
I can throw this ball so fast that it will fly back,
no parquet marks on it,
and land in your lap
crushing your manhood
and your upper plate and land
between your feet, teeth upward,
laughing at me.
This ball at least has holes I can dig into.
It is smooth and cool in my hands.
Its weight pulls on my upper arms,
but that's nothing compared to the heaviness in my heart.
49 years I have had to juggle around you
and never gotten a perfect score.
Go figure.
Where you got such nerve?
So, listen up buster…
I am throwing this ball
and its weight
means
nothing
to me
anymore.

April 9

The rain blankets the day
so the water rises, here and there
the cars stall in puddles
no camping,
it is Easter time, so
they all cram into the bookstore
like ants
busily hover over words
sharing favorite proverbs,
multicultural dichos,
not the oxfordwhitemale types
people reward themselves with good books
                                               on good Friday
words that ease
                    the holy day tense ness
mostly among family
the shadows linger and turn sour
                    on a day like good Friday,
                            we must
                    because we are Christians,
                    tend to our souls,
but alas,
who knows where to find the moment.

at times it feels cold
    the sun keeps hiding from me
    touching the glass figure
    i feel the cold

    holding him close
    in memory
    the sound comes out
    touching me
    touching...
    melting my fears away.

    does the sun warm
    soldiers at war
    can they be warmed
    by the sunshine that melts
    my fear away

    or do they feel not
    the beauty in the sun
    letting
    falling down to the grass
    they feel the warmth
    that the earth took away
    from the sun.

    smoke puffs fill the sky
    here and there thunders a gun
    letting
    falling down to the grass
    they feel not
    they hear not
    they kill not
    shall we pray?

    can we pray
    or have we forgotten how
    in the racing days
    there is no more time
    for such useless things

can you
how do you talk about how wrongs you have done
or is there no need for more talk
can you
without looking for him live
talk to him
he will come and ease your pain
through a returning soldier
greeted by flowers from a girl.

sons of sons will go to war
  for a mere façade
  how can we stop
  why can we not stop
  this endless trial

  praying will not cure the wounds
  that mothers have
  that soldiers have
  but the child will cry out
  where has my father gone?

  he is always with us
  cries the mother
  what else can she say
  but hold him close and pray?

Celebration of birth, a requirement
Dignity at death, denied
The winds of our times are blowing hard

It is the time for sorrow
for remembrance
that human to human
We are not
By ignorance or choice
The times are as such

Do you ask yourself
What is forest management
What is harvesting stem cells
What is killing mother's children for oil
What are hormones in our foods
What is air that is not air anymore
What is ice that does not melt and ice
That never melted that does melt
Who can you call to ask
Who can you call to ask but yourself

The baby food is homogenized
The sounds are homogenous
Or vice versa
The fact is that they are both tasteless
But Baby never knows the difference
But the eyelashes grow long
The mother's milk is unnecessary
Yet nature gives her best nourishments in it
Size three is a woman's test
Otherwise undesirable

I ask grandmother what has happened
And she blows the clouds to the west
Merciless is the answer

Only cockroaches can survive this
And you and I are left
Holding an empty self
All is demanded to be the same at a discount or else
You will not survive

Where is the compassion in
Sending humans to kill other humans
What has forsaken our kind that we are such

Code breaker

He was a piano player during the night war
he says and turns his head
We all stare at the back of his head
as he readies to untangle the keyboard
like
the drummer playing his beach necklaces
the twists, the gentle pull
the breaking of the codes
among books, that era has passed

The millions of Jews in ashes
haunt my memory
as I was not one of them
their soft, passive songs
life the spirited to high heaven even now
I cry to sleep over those lost souls
as they are reborn
in the drummer, the code breaker piano player
and in me.
The end of the line has been reached.
Mankind cannot do more wrong to me.
I am without child.

Count on nothing as your own,
You will never be disappointed

In the midst of abundance still yearning
For more and more, when there is enough
Just not knowing the limits of one's greed and need
For things to cover the wounds that have not been looked at
Examined for the fact that they are not needed
Any more.

No more of this or that.
Shake the "stuff" that hangs on your soul
Like leeches
It is not you. Just the blood needed
Yours, for other's journey
And you are left with stuff around you
Chaos to block the view to
Clarity of mind and one needs not a thing else.

What camel can go through this needle's eye
Jesus said that the poor will be there
Half a sentence it seems \ if we are the bearer of his truth
Why Why Why
We sing and go on to make another dollar to add
To our retirement not betterment of human kind
Where is the passion for truth, for searching for knowledge
Where is the art that stuns us to the truth of things
Who has forgotten to weigh in at this game and why

J Edgar Hoover feared
The words of Bea Richards
For the poems coming from her soul
threatened the government
Overthrow the leader with but a few lines of poems
He thought it so and was right
The power is still there
We must not be afraid to write them and allow them to see the light of day
We must encourage each other and be our best
This will not do for our grandchildren
Yours, not mine since I did not make them
My heart goes out to them and I shout to the sky
Behold the future, it is as such
And I pray to the God that I hold sacred
To stop the flow of destruction
It is that time.

Remember the young man at Tiananmen Square
There was a moment true to be human
Or my father in forced labor camp without
The world's attention on his acts
The same as Tiananmen Square call Recsk

Have we forgotten the strength
One
Person hold for a model to follow
Where have we lost our gutsiness to fight for
The right to be true to be human

All the same color
All the same one color
All the same ness
All the aimlessness seems the same now.

Watching people go by dressed in labels
Corporate advertisements, breathing into their life
Losing themselves
Losing hues of differences that make us one bright light

What is missing cannot be forgotten
What is here needs to be remembered
Never to be repeated again

What kind of future do we create for humans
With blind sight
With hindsight
With echoes not memories of what we were made of
Stardust from the same universe

What is the stardust made of, tell me that
What is humanly possible to understand
When the eyes are close to each other on your face
Where is the space needed to absorb and create
What beauty is demanded for a given life
That is what is given and taken so freely, without hesitation
A better car it seems is our goal lately

So far out we look in search of what we are made of
So short is our sight of what is within that makes us

Where is the balance
And when we see
The smallest possible part of ourselves

The answers elude us
Still the chemicals do not make us right
Still the mystery is the mystery
Yet we do not honor it
We do not give it joy or sorrow as it demands
We harvest the science and call it success
When all along the science leads us back to the mystery
Unexplained,

What can be explained is minor
What cannot be answered is the crux of everything

We can chant love and peace
We can write poems of grace
We can listen well enough
To know the truth in ourselves

Do not ignore the best, yourself and your truth.

Current Events

I am bleeding invisible blood.
the river catches my soul
and echoes.
I am disappearing
my friends are having fun
no one knows the pain i feel
I am not afraid of death
i am afraid of life
mankind has lost its senses
the forest have lost their strength
to hold back men the birds have stopped singing
of all but death
the monsoon is hitting India like every year
and the Mississippi is taking a wide run along the banks
the water supply is low at best
the horror movies are more horrific or without success
the two-year olds talk in longer phrases
with guns in hand and
dream-snails can barely move
at the pace they like the earth
is more defiant to them
the silkworm has stopped dreaming
the women have stopped weaving
dreamless or in-turned
the spirits have landed
on the wrong side of our beds.

do we all agree…?
…that
Nature
came before mankind.
Well then,
Nature first.

Say
No more war…no more war
no more war…no more war
and squint your eyes
and say no more war enough times
maybe
it will happen.

Asa Carter burns in hell
Little Tree sits, watching.

Dear Susan Sontag

The six o'clock news had your face and words
across the screen and I wondered
do you know that there are women,
artists, who had fled that land, Sarajevo
because most men are mad with war, here, too,
that wherever you decide to face, east or west, men
kill, maim and brutalize women
that no matter how deeply we bury our heads
it is there and will remain
until the last killer and kill-man-imitating woman
exhale their last breath.

I have walked this Earth for 44 years, learning that
the Chinese bind their daughter's feet to pleasure a suitor
and must walk behind the man.
The Hindis burn their young brides when the husband dies
and punish girls students for incorrect answers while learning.
In Malaysia, one must bow one's head below a man's head.
The Africans cut the clitoris of girl children.
The Hungarians rather not have children, if must,
a boy child is best. The Japanese dress their women funny
and rather not have them in their theatre
The Christians birth girl children, already in sin
with no redemption, unless in total submission to a man.
The Jews worship their women in their home, only.
The Arabs cover their women's faces and lock them up
so no other man can get a glimpse of their property.
The American male can rape and beat a woman with
hardly any punishment. The right to decide to bear someone's child
is illegal, making war is legal.
The woman child is unprotected.
As I look behind and weigh the odds,
it favors men, wherever we, the women, are.

How does a woman live and survive the odds
How does a thinking woman retain sanity
How do old women, mothers and grandmothers live to

watch their girl children suffer even after their own suffering ended.
Can any woman remain un angered in the deepest sense.
How does the sun get up each day to shine on all of us
How does the moon stream across the sky, stealing day's yawn
filling night's sleepy eyes, knowing the laws under them

When a baby is born, do they know the difference
do they come with such conditions in their heart
or do we, the women who raise them
Can love and desire for harmony un damage the child.
how can all our efforts go unheeded, for how long
for how long can this last.

"Not all mean are bad" who would ever think that but
I am tired of the changes, the patronizing sentences
"It is slow to come about," the change that is.
"Oh get over it, it is better than before"
"What's the matter don't you like men?"
"Are you one of those man-hating women," just because I ask.
"Are you a lesbian, can't get a man?" I smile.
by choice if not design
I raise my arms and shout
look back, look back, they burnt the witches
All the strong women are gone, I mourn now.
We are helpless in a world of technological
wonders, all for the men,
49% of the population, in this land.

Good men are hard to find, if found, they seem comfortable
in their empowered life, they are not leading the fight.
Should not these good men be among the leading feminists of our times?
I heard that Native American Medicine Men have said
"It is the power of the women that will redeem this world,
allow them to do their work."
Is it heard out there in la la land?
Could you send me good news from anywhere?

Driving on Tunnel Road

sidewalks without people
bus stop without benches or something to stand under in rain,
I looked at the woman waiting for the local bus in front of Trailways.
she was old and fragile, standing in the water run-off
waiting for the bus,
getting some rain gear out,
expecting it to pour down any time, soon.
The bus pulled up, surprised, it was full.
Old people black and white
no eco-minded yuppy here
we all sit in our own little cars
blackening the leaves,
the undersides are like chimneys
echoed by the soot
oh no never mind
the inside. the white side

the safety
hell of a factor for women
it is safe downtown, once again
we have taken back the streets day and night.

So where did we go wrong?
I have asked myself that for 20 out of 40 years
and the answer comes again and again:
those who need to control, with wee bits for penises
at the helm, in a stately prance,
will control you through the words of God
God did not write the Bible, HIS disciples did.
The book of Jesus is still a mystery.
God is a wisp,
a kindness that sparks between two people, lovers,
mothers and daughters, brothers and sisters,
a kindness that cannot be tainted by
Man in his trickery, twisting and preaching as he likes
because his passion is CONTROL that carries him away.

Yes, I defy your religion, Man,
Yes, I defy your laws upon my body.
Yes, I will take up arms and show
what can be done to you
as you have done unto me.
The gates have been opened.
God is not on your side.
You have abused all things too far,
too long,
too well.
God has grown tired of you,
MANkind.

My wish upon a star is for the human race to go extinct,
to save and not soil the rest of the universe.
This is how God has taught me to serve -
to die, to die for all of us
with a joyful heart,
to stop the plunder,
to stop the Deeres cutting cutting, more pegboard
for Betty's busy afternoons.

The sound of the rainforest is devoid of birdsong now.
The electric saw
that folds trees like grandmother

folds the laundry, buzzes in my dreams.
We learn to soil so early.
Throw your clothes on the floor, wear them only once,
use more water,
use more chemicals, good smells are important,
and not-to-cling most essential.

How can this be? Life that suffocates in order to survive.
Did Darwin see the whites of God's eyes?
The truth is that the white must go.
It is a color that is LESS, that lacks and sucks all dry.
Those not white must be washed, white-washed,
so as to not alert them to the blessings
of yellow, browns, blacks
yes those are of the earth.

And life is what we have.
The power is hot, stricken, like metal ready to bend,
the color comes and turns red,
yes,
one more bang,
the color we see and bend
will break
this ancient mold for eternity.

If God could write
and all we need to know
could fit in a book
what kind of a god do you thing she would be
and who would believe her.

If God could write
and all we need to know
fit in a book
you know that kind of God he is
and everyone believes him.

Rebellious words come after 504 phone calls

at first light, waiting, and breathing taboo
never really knowing WHO LAYS down the LAW
hearts that freeze others out of fresh air
hearts that trample on you while you are bleeding
while your bones shatter and scatter
that's how men of cloth like to see you
on your knees, OH
such forgiveness, lies the monster
blue skinned, erect, searching, forcing
air out of lungs of young girls
readying to be WIVES to good men
THIS will CLeanNse the soul, as told
HOLD the SECRET, HOLD the SIN…
amen.

THE PHONE CALLS CAME.
………………………………….."weobjecttohomosexualsusingpubliclandsforstaterally" we should burn them, such evil children we burned the witches, we can do it again.

Three Rabbits: a fable
by Zoltan Zelk
retold from Hungarian by Emöke

One upon a time a long long time ago
a gathering of three Rabbits took place
in the middle of the Deep Deep forest
upon silver grass, they sat for awhile
maybe only for an hour, they sat and chewed
morning fresh dandelions. After a while they decided to go home
when a crow flew above them in the summer sky
and cried out to them "What you you all up to?
Like Lords you sit on your thrones.
What are you all up to, three Rabbits?"

"True, just like Lords we are–"
answered the three Rabbits
"and from now on we shall be like Lords
and eat only crow meat for lunch.
Never shall we waste time.
Right now we begin our crow hunt."

The silly crow believed the three Rabbits
and flew in haste spreading the news…
calling all other animals' attention
to the plans of the three Rabbits
and this is what the crow said to the fox

"Imagine, I am on my morning flight
minding my own business and as I pass the big
poplar tree in the Deep Deep forest,
you know the place,
in the middle of that meadow with the silver grass
I see Three GIANT Rabbits in high council.
They are bigger than bears

and I asked them what they were planning so seriously
and you know what they said?
They said that they are planning their lunch
and from now on only fox meat will satisfy them."

This is no joke, thought the fox to himself,
I better get out of here!
I certainly do not want to be lunchmeat!
The fox started to run towards the edge of the Deep Deep forest
where safety was awaiting him in his fox hole.
As the fox was running for dear life he crashed into the wolf
"HO HO, slow down, who set fire to you fox?"
"Imagine, I am on my morning hunt
minding my own business and as I pass
that big poplar tree in the Deep Deep forest,
you know the place,
in the middle of the meadow with silver grass
I see Three Giant MONSTER Rabbits in high council
they are bigger than bears,
and I asked them what they were planning so seriously
and you know what they said?
They said that they were planning their lunch
and only wolf meat would satisfy them.
You better run yourself and fast, if you value your life.
Imagine, their teeth TWO feet in length,
three fierce Rabbits, I tell you, run for your life."

That is all the wolf needed to hear.
He ran so fast he left the fox behind.
He ran towards the due of the Deep Deep forest
where is cave stood nearby
and ran right into a bear.

"HO HO, who set fire to you wolf?"
"Imagine ear, I am out on my walk
minding my own business as I pass
the big poplar tree in the Deep Deep forest,
you know the place,
in the middle of the meadow with silver grass
I see Three FIERCE Giant Monster Rabbits in high council

they are bigger than dinosaurs,
and I asked them what they were planning so seriously
and you know what they said?
They said that they were planning their lunch
and only bear meat would satisfy them.
Imagine, their teeth THREE feet in length,
three Fierce Rabbits, I tell you, run for dear life."

That is all the bear needed to hear.
He ran after the wolf, the fox not too far behind them.
They ran so fast that not even the North Wind could catch up to them.
In their haste they did not notice the hunter approaching them.
They all ran so hard that they almost ran him down.
The hunter had never seen such a sight.
They caught him off guard and to his amazement
they all shouted to him
"Run, run for your life, hunting Man!
Imagine, we are on our morning hunt
trying to avoid one of your bullets
and we come upon the big poplar tree in the Deep Deep forest,
you know the place,
in the middle of the meadow with silver grass
I see Three FIERCE GIANT MONSTER Rabbits in high council.
We asked them what they were planning so seriously
and you know what they said?
They said that they were planning their lunch
and only hunter meat would satisfy them.
Imagine, their teeth FOUR feet in length.
We tell you, run for your life!"

The hunter was beside himself.
Never had he seen such an event.
A fox, a wolf, and a bear running for their lives.
This must be serious.
He certainly did not want to be lunchmeat.
He turned on his heels faster than lightning
throwing his rifle in the bushes along the path.
He swore to himself that he would never hunt again,
as long as he lived, if he made it back to his house
safely, near the edge of the Deep Deep forest.

The afternoon Sun finds the three Rabbits in their den
doing rabbit things like twitching their whiskers,
thumping the ground, nudging each other,
flopping ears, and yawning after an afternoon nap.
One parent rabbit bakes a dandelion puff pie
the other parent collects watercress and wild sorrel
for their afternoon delight.

                                      The End

Life, your life and mine
demands never less of an act from each,
you and me.

The hour is past midnight
Thoughts are rushing through my mind
What else can I say to wake us out of slumber
What else can I do but make the books available
For learning and expanding the universe within
My father chose the sword as I choose the power of words
To throw light on our path
We will ever know we were born to be the light
We will ever know that we are the stars of our lives
We will ever grace each other in passion's sight

Hoping for one morning when we awaken together and
Shift this paradigm into nothing less
Than what the creation demands
Of the goodness that is in humans
That we are capable of
We need to see it now
We need to look again
We need not to expect the same
We need to not accept the same
We have seen the worst by now
We have tasted fruit with no taste at all
Cold and a bit sour, refrigerated
unlike the apples in Paradise
That Adam and Eve quenched their thirst with
And started our life
outside the garden but
Still within God's sight.

Bloodlines

A present from my sister

you gave me a recorder

handmade

i touched the holes

bringing songs that we both know

you, like a child demanded more

asked for one that none has heard

and I obeyed

gave you my own soul,

have you heard?

A spider bit me

That night that the spider bit me
I dreamt of marching soldiers
Skinny legs, spider bellied
Metal shields in their left hands,
Shielding their bodies like old women

That night the spider bit me
I remember best the horse that laughed
The oven that receded only
The carrot that grew purple
Tasting like wild sorrel
I remember best, you
cradling where it was swollen
On that night
a spider bit me and
You became a man

The car, the car is not here, where is my car,
our car, the one we have, the keys to it, will you get it for me?

At eleventhirty pm
sitting on his bed, one leg touching the floor,
full of pain, the other missing for two years now
my father sits, covered with sweat
whispering out of memories, when he was a full-bodied man.

Old age is a curse they say,
I can see it now from a distance
not so far, my beloveds are heading into it
full of courage with a monstrous head
the fear resides at moment
when they see the difficulties for all of the children
when the tongue can not find the right words
when the forgotten are the tasks that were everyday events.

I keep chanting to my mother, who is strong like granite
disguised in a fragile body
when the fear straddles too close to her
I come chanting to her, it's ok I am here with you
we will tackle this too
you have been all your life alone.

I remember when I was seven
looking into the only mirror we had
taking the vow, the commitment
I am her defender, her warrior child
through thick and thin, through loss and sorrow
I am here just for her and that is enough for my lifetime.

I want so much to keep old age afar from them

to gentle their path
to receive the gifts that they bestow upon me
just with the presence
the lessons we never taught give gifts
I have been waiting for
accept my present with a glad heart.

The sun set each night with a crowing glory
turning us into the house, into our hearts
and as each night I lean to kiss each of them
I know I am alive and present
ready each morning to begin again.

April 2nd 1964, La Havre France

The train ride from Paris to La Havre
                                       unmemorable

The expectations of the ocean crossing
                                       enormous

the expectation so freeing my father
after eight years of separation
                                       indescribable

SS America was the name of the oceanliner
we were embarking on to arrive in
                                       New York City, America

leaving Budapest and grandparent behind

I had never seen the ocean before
I had never even see a large body of water
except Lake Balaton
which we called our "ocean"
in a country the size of Indiana

The boarding for the oceanliner
                                       chaotic
The photographer caught our picture
                                       like frightened birds
The steps down to our minuscule cabin
                                       suffocating
The window to the outside
                                       round and small

Mother tried to keep us close at all times
but my sister and I were ready
to explore

off we went
without words we expressed
sights of everything unfamiliar

holding our breath and each other's hands
the harbor still within reach

In the middle of the night
the oceanliner left the continent
Leaving all we knew behind.

Before breakfast
we walked out to see the ocean
holding each other's hands

forever
breathtaking
limitless
endless
blue grey
windworn
frightening
paralyzing

speechless we stood by the railing
holding our breath and each other's hands

Leaving Budapest and grandparents behind
Silence in our hearts
endlessly
the sound of waves
reached and sealed a knowing
no turning back!

black to the blind

beads covering his way

i show him my colors

he can see them

those that came to see

never saw the light

we must go on

freedom as a bird

traveled with us

crowds came to see   us

they have not seen the colors

sleepless nights

covered with snow

I was going down the road

the blind man was still there

long ago, he told me the colors

that i only saw through his eyes

our father was not there at all.

below shadows, time sneaked by

stealing love's lonely keepers

for i am not where he is

for all we are, we are not yet.

the sun came up from the east

birds hanging on to air

they will not let go

why people let go, ask not the birds.

A Wednesday morning asleep yet meditation called the birds awake like a tonal adjustment they came first on the right the response from the other side I felt like the first morning in awe of their greetings the miracle of being and the gentling of their music it is the birds that fly away with our souls and come the stork for renewal

I want to remove the I want from me she said. What an assignment she accepted. Distraction, money the need for it are against you. This society is not capable of worshiping anything but the money. I can feel the eyebrows raising by many who feel they are with religion but what about having faith? It is not a society that is filled with grace or faith. It is not a society that forgives or allows transgression with mercy. It is a society where the bigger and the have mores dispose and rule over the rest. What gracelessness brings out is the worst in man.

My eye sight is going. The 30 years of reading and straining have taken their tolls. Oh, to be without the ability to read is a frightening thought. I can type because I know the keyboard intimately. It is the keyboard that allows me to write so you too can read these words of thoughts flickering through my mind. Why do I write to you, the reader? I frantically want to find the words to make you understand that we do not have that much time for frivolous mis understands. It is the earnest desire to get you to pay attention to the lives that we are leading. Where this leads is not a safe place or pleasant at that. We as human beings are running short of time. Listen to your feelings allow the moment to permeate your soul.

What do I need to make my living worth while and productive, she asks over and over again.
The symptoms are there, follow the signs.
Time off to be able to get enough time for my mother and myself.
a desk and a person to ease my connection to the bookstore.
Time off to write my thoughts down and translate others' words cross cultural pollination. Strength comes from that.

Unseen or unknown colors you present to readers who weave the tapestry of our lives. We thank you for all the un named hues that allow us to be better persons. The knots we tie are unscheduled and never done before, a stronghold for our progression. I never thought I would be up here standing in front of you and be allowed to express my gratitude to be part of this process we call bookselling. I never thought my luck would lead me here. So here I stand tongue untied thanking you for your words and thanking you all for your work in spreading the words. I am glad to be part of this process we call bookselling.

earlier dream, late august 95
notes I took at 3:10 a.m as I woke up from dream

Papa in concentration camp, trying every which way to help him escape.
Developing code words
writing on the wall
"bread bread bread, if you want help"
tried to get in through the chimney exhaust pipe to save him from cremation
Asked for a cigarette non chalantly at a restaurant
will he swallow cigarette, burned me instead.
Priests tried to discredit me as an Asian or Aryan.
No matter what I tried I could not free Papa.
Rail road, beach
thinking if I left the car there as a decoy wand went on foot
maybe I could help him get out.
Deb Cris and Roberta were there to help me.
Roberta brought instructions from Deb on code language.

October 9
dreaming
Linda showing me how to rest, lie down and not her round but whenever I do it is rocks and uncomfortable
she keeps telling me and showing me how to take a break.

November 1
I woke from the dream because it seemed so real. I went to Hungary and lost my way in the subway. I found Ladin and told her that I am not writing and could not tell her that I am not translating. She had her bags packed I was afraid she was ready to come home with me. I did not want to bring her with me. We rode the subways for a while. She got me to the part ten on Gogol and a young man was there, living there with Andras who was at work. Left him a note. Ladin told me she still lived with Balint. who is Balint? I think finally I got back to the house were Papa and Grandma were.

It is my 47th birthday. I feel funny about it. Why is that I wonder. I feel Fake? Fake in what? I feel real in my life, I feel vulnerable at work. I feel fake as a writer, and translator. I am lost in a fog of no direction. I feel hopeless? Do I feel manipulated? So what? Life is manipulating my self on a hidden course. What is my agenda? Who cares and where is it going? Big ifs and no place to get a firm response. Why do I look to others to validate my life? Is this what Papa's problem was? All that direction and energy and no where to go? Where did he want to get to and why did he not? Did he accomplish his dream to work towards? Bigger store, bigger sales, more staff? Is that the dream? What do I want? Why don't I know what I want? It is a good dream to have the best store in the world? Why oh why? Keeping this body is fun. I do enjoy my daily life. I need to have my dream back, an active and every day thing so I don't loaf around aimlessly.

An elderly gentleman

April 7th, a Thursday morning,
the bookstore half-asleep.

The first customer reached the counter and smiled.
A bird like man, eyes friendly and knowing,
he accepted my greeting and began to dance.
His steps furtive as he hurried along the parquet floor.
He seemed to remember that books had importance in his life.
Author's names escaped him,
but he knows he wanted a book.
Several times, he returned to breathe the air of books
to be among friends, to try again.
His face was shaven but clumps of hair remained at places
around his lips and neck,
to remind me that he lived alone.
His jacket striped,
his slacks of an unmatching pattern, the tie and the shirt a cacophony
that witnessed the silence about him.

An elderly gentleman broke my heart today.
I kept thinking of my father in his last six months of life,
when he still made an effort to be himself,
to take care of his own business, half successful,
half forgotten. It did not matter after that
because mother was there to ease him into himself-
The smiles and the effort, then and now,
to do and be
moved stones around my heart.

I tried to engage him in conversation but he know
and remembered that he was not himself.
Irate at me, and at his inability to remember what he wanted,
he remembered to be frustrated,
so he left me
standing in the bookstore aching for something
I have not yet recalled.

Bernadette Bori

it was the season of the hearts
when I heard you were ill

I felt immediately scared
being without you laughter
and the inquisitive looks

you always bringing your questions

"where did I do that
how did I get that done
why did I not say things that needed to be said"

calling on my responsibilities
without which
none of us learn their own lessons

you
made me know you in an instant
you said the same
to your mother in explaining our connection
third cousin on my mother's side
you made us connect
you made me laugh
you made me cry
you.

Cousin Kis Ilonka

new like a bay lamb
hard to walk but soon enough even
the rain won't touch their skin
she was 52 years old,
bright and always on the play before her
illness
we, in the family,
never expected her to die young,
she laughed in all our faces
all my life she never looked back,
fast tracking to Moscow
and all those other politically
hot places she screeched through the sky
and now faded only in memory she shines.
the last time I saw her she knew
it was the last time.
she kept her eyes on me
and the light was shining through.
I knew it too. silently she gave me her
daughter
to take care of. already in a dream
she approached me 5 years before and
asked me to take my inheritance.
to be entrusted with that sweet burden of a
child
is always a delight to be needed
in the universe by another human life
to be connected with a thread.

    elongated shadows
          of the sun

make love to the earth
      my mother

      the sun
      my father

hidden lumps of dreams forgotten
mother
      do not give them up
he will warm you   anywhere
           anyway
sun and earth, my parents
i am of the universe
clouds are my dreams
the sky is my mind
the waters are my tears
your cars
      speeding south on
      ininetyone
      connecticut turnpike
are my children
of mutated technology
my wounds
      are your wars
the flowers among my hair
so softly sway
when the wind blows
when i whisper in your dreams

earth,
    my mother

sun,
    my father

  do not give up your dreams.

Forced Labor-death Camp Recsk, 1950 to Fall of 1953

In silence, his thoughts and memories remain
No, I do not want to talk about that time
Like a mantra
With alcohol breath. hallow eyes
He repeats under his breath
I do not want to talk about that time
And denies himself release,
Fragmented life
Imprisoned for life
800 of them.

Father, like a sleeping giant-volcano
His life, the pain and torture
Vibrated in every bone and the flesh
He does not cry out now or then.

The stories of good deeds
Come like bullets when they are gathering to visit
Survivors from the labor death camp
…and try not to talk about that time,
But never is it without the shards embedded…
Remember how B'Raćz called the guards'
Attention on himself…time and time again
He knew his limits and did his most
To careen the pain and punishment
Away from his frail and sick friends
Serving for no reason, without judgment
In this forced labor death camp called Recsk.

Kistarcsa, Recsk or Siberia
The Gulags sapped young men
Of strength and vitality
Sickness, nightmares and physical abuse
Remained to remind them of the era
We do not talk about
We do not know about
We cannot imagine, why, how.

Nations punished those who stood against the tide
Crimson, black, bile green souls
Enjoyed their power with guns at their side
The guards walked around like ghouls
Sowing their fear…here take that, and that.
No food for a week
Stand in water
Naked in December
Hands tied behind backs, shackled
Now take that.
Another month in solitary
Again and again,
His cries remained silent and self-contained.

Basalt mine, cracked hands, pick-axes flying
Bodies falling out of line
He picked them up daily and carried them
Back to their bunk bed, gave them his food
Acted up to direct the punishment on himself
Endlessly
The whip came down on his shoulders
That held his son gently…years later

The sun burned their backs
mining basalt in the quarry
everyday for three and a half years

The poems written by Faludy, were
committed to memory by Nyeste
when needed to be written down
in their blood, no ink to be had,
toilet paper needed to be stolen, he stole it

Got a week outside in a ditch
The capillaries in his ankles died
Years went by and seven amputations later
He died. He took the bad breath of an era with him
Without spreading it onto his children
Silently he went
Even then.

There was only one time father opened up
Only once the alcohol loosened his lips
They beat me so bad that
…I did not know if I was a boy or a girl…
And he laughed a short breath
That was under the Parliament before they took me
To the forced labor death camp.
To give your youth for Democracy
Is what was called for and was taken.

Fear for lack of power ruled the time and the land
The villagers near by knew and looked the other way
And even today the smell of the shame lurks in their hearts
Even today, the ghosts of Recsk haunt the hillsides.

A National Park now, commemorating 800 lives given
Destroyed for a moment of indecision of government
School children pile out of buses and cannot imagine
What was given for their freedom in Recsk.

Andrassy Ut 60 was the beginning torture chamber
That is now a museum in Budapest called the Terror Haz.
My mother and I went, stood in line for hours three times
We entered and faced oil snaking around a tank, black mirror
Reflecting all the mesmerized faces
And the room where they hung them upside down from a hook in
The ceiling is intact, beating them with water hoses full blast
Pulling the nails of their hands and feet
The hot iron that was used for prodding
All displayed like still in use for
Branding animals…their cries were still in that air
My mother and I ran out of the room breathless
Knowing what went on in there, brought it to life with such force
For both of us 40 years later
The solitary tomb was no bigger than a cave for a midget
The father that came out of there was a ghost of himself
He shielded his children from the pain and suffering he knew well
The toys and the bread on the table every day
We could not imagine
We did not know this man's past

And understood less what sent him into fury.
In our childish ways we expected everything
Brightness, happiness, good health for the man we held as our father.
The time was cut short for us to get to know
What was and remains buried in the past.
Buried but there too the guard on duty,
Armed and ready
To shoot on a whim, at any movement.
Fragmented life, like the quarry they worked, rocks
Frozen in time, gray and cold to touch
His life held in Prison
Even when the era was gone
We cannot imagine ever…
We will not understand ever…
We do not talk about
We do not know about
We cannot imagine
Man's inhumanity to man.

Grandpa Henry

Grandfather always whistled a particular hymn
when he wanted us to help in the garden.
The first tomato, luscious red
the first yellow pepper, a breath of angel's hair
canary yellow behind his back, the sun
he stood proud.

The first fruit, or berry is always his gift to us.
We run and like birds in the nest
behold the lingonberries, the plums,
quinces that still bring forth water
without words Grandfather would reach out
delighted while we picked
he would be telling a story.
My sister and I would sit in deep green grass under the willows
surrounded by peepers.

From under his reddish mustache
words would escape
intoxicating me, in his garden
I ate his words and the berries
and had no fear.

Change that adds up wrong, makes little holes and great love

fifteen neetfin ifften
bigger boogger baby
left a hole in iffteen's heart
treat alert neetfif.

nine babies plus 6 holes
will add up to chaos
fifteen neetfif without ifften
lacks 7 holes from glory.

never neetfif your 9 iffents
for nothing eentiff can do
shall be a greater hole
than the one you remember
in your grandmother's mittens
and she was the biggest love
mittens, holes and all.

The house that still stands

The telephone rang
Your voice filled with laughter
how unlike my Mother.
I listened.
Doors opened, you invited me
to share in the laughter and joy.

We talked of everyday intimacies
like we were not different.
The river is wide
anxious of the crossing
we eyed each other from distant shores
casting lies, aware of winds and currents
holding images, bridging the air blue
a hint of desire to connect.

Mother's work is never done
daughter's work has just begun
I hummed in silence, to myself.

"I wrote a poem" you said
my world has exploded
to befriend one's mother
to trust one's daughter
I am blessed.
We live in a house that still stands, Mother.

Hungarian childhood

1950
The knocking came at midnight in winter time,
the room was warm and at peace in the night.
Two men brought in the cold under their hats,
grabbed most of the books and threw them into sacks.
My father silent and unresistant,
like fallen leaves caught in a storm.
The silence was broken by echoes of sobbing after they left,
as the void spread and filled the room.
My father disappeared and from that moment on
a sense of lacking for what seemed like a century
we managed.

1953
Father walked back into our lives.
We started over with fear along our bedside.
The days and nights were filled with danger yet precious
as our father read us into sleep.
The epic poems he read us gave us the thread, the continuity.
Then it began again, the fear, the tanks.
The calendar marked 1956 now.
My answer to all that was playing hard,
not eating the spinach, not drinking the milk,
playing hard at being a child and to forget.
The butterfly's last dance frantic,
I came to rest on my mother's ironing board
he left- is all she said.
I remember the void in her eyes, the cold around my heart.

1957
Grandparents, like missionaries came,
bathed us in loving thoughts,
showing the way, singing songs.
The laundry flew high on the line, the vegetables tasted like life.
Now 1963, the steam roast above the ironing board
the radio was on, an opera, my sister and I were hanging around,
my mother humming the aria, the continuity

interruption in the broadcast…
President Kennedy assassinated.
The fear has not left since then
the iron cooled off, the board was put up.
The opera, resumed without mother, passports in hand
we crossed the continent and the ocean to start again.

1964
The man at Pier 82 was my father, they said.
Eight years have passed.
Begin again. Begin at being a family again
look ahead…learn a new language…start a new life.
Old clothes that needed ironing replaced by drip and dry…
new machines…new sounds occupied our newly fantastic life.
Cries of a boy-child filled my heart,
hope and flight…new friends and fast cars hurried those years by.
I left the little girl behind without goodbyes,
to face a new nation, to face a language anew.
I searched and search for what, I still do not know.

1991
My father returned to Hungary, mother alongside.
The medal was pinned on his chest, we wept,
standing in the parliament he was speechless.
Fear has no hold on us any longer, it took all we had.
No we that we stand watching time eat us, one by one
from where we came, so we shall return.
Without government, without religion, without your parents,
lovers, brothers, sisters…there is nothing else.
The fear, the despair encircles me and without answers
I try remembering myself, a new herself, a childhood.

Ides of March

The Ides of March, again.
He closed the door on himself.
The shutting-out now seem inevitable.
A youth, my father gave to his country
and never looked back.
Alcohol sits thick on his breath
although he never smells it himself.
Each next day is a new day as
he paints windows on the four walls.
His son, the only reflection,
carries his name, a burden of family names
the fame that has faded and now returns to
throw the light on the truth that still stands.
A country sits heavy on a son's shoulders.

Motherland, such a cruel lover.
She holds you afar yet draws in the heart.
The heart that beats with each moment for no other,
is lead along a road going nowhere.
Mirage on the flatland.
Such a cruel lover, Motherland.

Forty years sits on her shoulders, the daughter,
one who can never make the impact that rivers demand
where her words fall, like leaves in the winter on now-covered land
in silence, the echo strikes blue. No one hears her thunder.
Such a cruel lover, Motherland.
The tears become rivers that nurture new lands.
To the mind, her only true possession, she has fled.
She holds the olive branch, touching the ground, where she heads.
She holds no answers in her hands, she bows her head
before her Motherland, such a sweet lover.

La boheme, a color chosen while blinded

We are orphans at the train station
unsure of the destination
fingers cramped and blue
eyes round and expectant.
A mix of nature, mystery and fact.
Taste of lavender tugs at my soul
the color of tears at her grave.
I feel her words:
Begin without your Grandmother
Go forth with flashing lights in your hair
Allow the strength and the violet to speak, grow
like clouds before a storm in the making.

On the telephone with my mother

I told my dream on the phone
you said
"how miraculous dreams are"
and neither of us dreamt that night.

Mother, I am not you
for not a single moment am I without you.
In my heart I plead for you to see that
happiness is in your hands.

I want to look you in the eyes
and command you to be happy.
I lift the veil so you are able to see
three children
your creations, dreaming of your happiness.

The veil is lifted.
It is through the struggle
that happiness tips her hat.

moments just moments turn into year in a wheelchair
waiting for the morning coffee to arrive
when they have the time not when I need it or just plain want it
they say I could go get it myself
how my hands hurt when I touch the wheels
my shoulders burn when I turn the wheels
how come I suffer so much
how come pain is my constant companion.

get ready for another day
get dressed
wash face, teeth
the burden of facing another day
the burden of moving the foot, the arms
the mind like a speedboat on a quiet lake
speeds out of control
sleep evades me in the dark
eyes get blurred when reading
the mind endlessly chases itself around the teeth
at a slight tremble

the sun plays on the leaves
like flowers opening to the warm light
they reach for the sun only if you stay very still.
do notice the movements of the leaves.

You can smoke in heaven.

In a row, clad in black
the sky beneath their feet
sat 2 women, a man, 3 women
in a row, my kinfolk.
Their feet resting on clouds
my dream began.

I stood behind them, arms folded.
The right foot furtive, fidgeting
in a room with no walls
encapsulated, soundless.

My grandmother stood to my left
in a paisley patterned dress
smiling, cigarette in her left hand.
"You can smoke in heaven"
is all she said
and smiled at me.

I jolted out of bed
and said "thanks".
My first visitation from my grandmother
January 20, 1922

Grandmother died last year.

A love so distant

my hand holds a book
it is hard covered filled with poems
this hand that holds a book
holds not man's hand
it turns the white jacket
the ink smears since its wetness
red and black
the yellow
like Grandmother's skin
shirts green
through the photograph
I reach madness
a love so distant falls through the crack in my hands.

Nature

Affi8nity in Nature

Observe and understand the working of affinity in Nature...
                    Ada to Ruby in Cold Mountain

1.
I was born because...
you might begin your own story
and this thought will lead you
                    entertain you
for the journey we call life.

How much we learn, share, reject
                accept
                    turn onto different paths
we think a change in direction of our own choosing
wild chance at birth can still only a change at life.

Is it carved in your bones
                out of your soul
where and when the stars glimmer their dreams
or nightmares in your cosmic
soup and
your reaction is a physical nature
the laws of the body
forever hungry at best?

A chance at fission and fusion
already millions and millions
of opened and closed windows
one two
one two
those are the choices, yes?

Is what we call a life, given
our minuscule minds,
dance a spiral waltz
or a rope hesitant
without hope of a net?

The body sooner or later comes to a rest, an affluent of glands and fats, it
thinks I'll go this way (if you insist) for awhile,
stretching that ever so fragile thread
to a point of demise and the break, yes (no return ticket), is
a violent force
that will out cast the stones of David and Goliath

It is the arrogance of the mind
that the ego eats up for sustenance day
and night. The ego needs the visible self
that only remains inside between
the first hoot and the last howl of the night

2.
observe the dogwood
red berries among the green leaves
the birds eating the fruit
seeds travel to give the seed
that chance to grow, to be
a sight of beauty, another dogwood tree

observe that dogwood tree
that is does not grow to be the tallest
and resemble an apple tree in bloom.
when the redbirds cast the seeds
away on the soil fertile, they are helping
things that need to travel,
seeds that yearn
for another shoreline of a creek.

observe the dogwood tree
becoming
symbolic of holy acts and facts
another way outside of its own nature
beauty's importance in the chance
to survive and beautify
otherwise we pay no attention.

observe the dogwood

the poisonous pulp of rhododendrons,
the way of protection.
confuse the master plan
two-legged careless
invaders of the land and its beauty

observe the dogwood tree,
observe the red berries,
observe the birds, carrying red berries away
here and there
where the dogwood finds itself the place.

A dog barks at morning dew.

3.
Arms resting under my head,
breath nourishing my dreams.
Eternity looks for me.

Your arm curves round my body,
our thighs touching.
Sleep is dazzling our consciousness.

Open like the morning sky
light folds round our doodie's and minds.
You are a are a bubbling spring.

A snail elopes with the moon.
An orchid opens, purple hues.
The sky yawns the morning into existence.

A branch without leaves, the moon
dancing among the star dust.
Time folds herself, again.

I hear my name called-
unfamiliar voice, a calling of
unknown origin- in a dream.

The wind claims the mountains.

Yellow river roils through clouds.
The view never remains constant.

The challenge remains constant.
The results vary.
I stand against time, head bowed.

Your other arm rests on the pillow.
Your dreams hold me close.
Slowly, you climb into my dreams.

Toes touching the sole of your feet.
Cats perch by your head.
Sleep has you in her grip.

4.
A siren writes her verse in blood.
Shallow waters serve up fish.
The feast is always in your honor.

Tangerine yellow covers the sky.
Purple follows her into the night.
I greet the morning among your branches, dark blue.

Your eyes light blue.
Your hair yellow like winter straw.
A red ladybug on my keyboard.

Hours sit by my left,
room enough for twilight on my right.
I scream into silence.

The dog barks, the ladybug traverses my desk.
I sink into a cloud of smoke-
you, my love, are afar.

I recall the hint in your eyes
reminding me that we are one.
We dance to dreams yet to come.

5.
Money, mother said, you make so little.
I worry about you when I'm gone,
otherwise I would not ask.

Money to be made is soul to be sold.

Twenty years a labor of love.
Armed with finely printed tomes
I cross every road.

You are a sprite with a strangeness of beauty.
You are a gift of love.
I now stand tall.

The mulberry tree with silken leaves
trembles at my thoughts.
The snail takes hours from my life as I watch.

Oh, where is the ladybug? My eyes dart from
oh, which cup. O, yes, the French Broad Food Co-op.
A drop of red in water.

Just in time I save the ladybug from drowning.
She moves joy through my heart.
Lavender yellow.

That moment I describe no coin can by.
I want to write, left to right-
always the search goes on.

Nail-biting time, you know the feeling,
like nettles, lining up for the thrill.
Three crows with piece of bread.

6.
My father came down from heaven,
a visit,
the first in five years.

He said-
he has been there for me for fifty years.
Tai chi and chamomile tea he recommends for tears.
A woman of 75 years searches for…reasons.
Fear still gripping her soul, my mother is
a butterfly caught in a spider web.

She tries again and again to be free.
She call more and more question to reason.
The spider approaches at leisure.

She feels a closeness, up and to the left in her eyes.
Her glimpses yield nothing to be sure of.
One wing becomes tired an falls agains the web.

Movement is essential to the present.
Movement becomes a prisoner in the present.
The past rides by, she smells it and remembers.

Waiting bores the butterfly. Patience makes her slip.
The current of the movement sets her free.
Her children hunger for her still, her given strength.

A pelican glides above, a dolphin swims by, a sunrise
busts the morning sky open-
gifts of hope and love color the horizon.

We sit by the oven, searching for sharks' teeth and shells.
My mother and I measure time together,
counting between the thunder and lightning.

A walk toward the house bewitches the weather.
It clears and we laugh with the honestly of children.
Ten more days beckon us towardd ourselves.

Yellow impatiens and blue bog grass adorn
the entrance, shouting of late spring.
Rocks hold the soil in place, readying for rain.

At three a.m. palms hide in the shadow of the night.
A five a.m. they become visible.
Silence fills the streets with promise of a new day.

The wind brings old branches to the ground.
The palm trees recognize freedom.
What surprise is in the un noticed loss that renews.

7.
The heat shrivels the leaves.
The roots reach for moisture.
I wait for the rain to come.

By the shallow river
we meet again.
You sit among the branches, singing.

autumn comes with fiery steps
       hands playing with hot and cold
       so many days filled with
       the coming of fall's closing eyes

       hatless, running to meet the wind
       hair like so many leaves
       flutter with the song of fall
       music of rain colors your days
       nights
       the moon wearing winter coat
       of clouds gathering throughout
       spring and summer days
       winter is to come
       bringing
       snow
              ice
                        cold
       warmness
                        to hearts
                        remembering summer colored rain.

be the pig and eat only the best morsels
dig for the truffles

like the camel quench your thirst
only when there is clean water

like the lion roar when hungry
warn the night of your coming

like the mouse fit anywhere
eat anything

like the snake
stand firm and strong

like the spider
write words against the morning dew.

Blue ant in yellow box

After seeing Mindwalk, the movie

give a page a name
give a street an address
find the next sunset
find the next angel
the windkimmers, the spirits
that playfully lift your skirt
the ones that always play in leaf piles
they flirt with energies, unspoken, bottomless
the mind walks on the keyboard
knowing that it is not mount saint michel
the physicist the poet and the politician
like the poet and the monk
the respect extended
the bow in the head signifies
yes i am willing to listen
keep the thread
i want to weave with you.

Atomic

holding muchmore less
fingers
opening
closing
gravitational
universe contained
precipitates.
The hot crucible gained weight
should have evaporated
powerless water drops
splitting into bombs.
The smaller
the bigger the split.
The closer
the farther it hits.

Breathing

The rocks speak to me.
They jump out of the earth, surprised me again
yet the ground is closed and solidly defies the movement.

Writing is a spiritual path, your own
Carolyn Forche said
It requires discipline.

Millions of ants approach me.
I am laying down in the grass, spotted with rocks, hard
My eyes close to the ground, belly down
My left arm supports my upper body, poised over the paper
My fingers touch my left breast,
the sun lazily catches a glimpse of the sky
noticing a cluster of mole mounds, soft and upturned
without resistance
I sense the difference in textures
it seems natural, not frightening
the differences that contain the self I call myself.

Earth, rocks, mole mounds, ant and my body
attached to the ground not falling into the sky
the sun plays catch me if you can among the leaves
and on top of quartz specks
Safe, I observe myself
protected
Earth, herself
for the moment is right here and now.
I hear Marnie's voice - I give you permission
to roll in the grass like you used to as a child and
don't forget to laugh
dig your face, connect to the Mother
exhale and intake all it is that is given

Craggy Gardens

The beginning needed eyes
a moon
swinging in space,
and four branches.
When your body was added
it made life
a newness for each day
four moments
to spark the moon
to sing lullabies for you.
just for you.

The bear
steps on the branches, crushing them
its fur darkly deep
the breath racing from its snout
I do not run away
I stand still to invisible.

To see a beginning,
the bear,
majestically
rises above the horizon
its eyes, the stars, black as coal.
The cold wind disfigures my head
shrinking,
as the sky falls away.
I am on top of the world.
It is Craggy Gardens at full moon,
above everything, I stand.
The clouds fill the crevices below me
passing time.

the deer
  in touch

soft brown eyes
so moist
  are the lips

above the ground
  erect
alert to the silence in the night

the deer
  in touch with the meadow

knows all silences and rustles

the quiet air lingers

one alerting sound from miles

the deer will spring forth

losing track of time

into safe distance
  silence
    she will take.

hollyhock humming bird
deep purple rose
salt
tree trains
yellow socks
yellow pillow
train trees
salt
sausage bread
deep purple rose
yellow trains
humming birds
yellow yellow
pillow pillow
tree train tree
willow willow

How the mountains bow to each sunset
How the hummingbird approaches the flower
petals, drenched with dew, awaiting harvest.
Laden with pollen, the flower sighs.
The hummingbird drinks the nectar
drunk, she flies.

To love myself
I observe the hummingbird.

I watch the casts lick each other, shiny clean.

The dog, my ankle in her mouth gently
the tail wagging.
The dog likes me, I should too
but doubt creeps back through the crowsfeet on my face.

I search everywhere for clues to who I am.
Loving myself is a faint possibility,
I can tell not when I am found yet.
Is this really a question to ask
isn't being and living enough
maybe if I held a mirror to the self
I would be brave enough to look
and see.
What is bravery?
Who took it from me
or did I give it away and not notice?
Do I even want it back?

I owned my farm two years before I learned that

Snakes prefer green velvet couches.
Spiders weave the most beautiful webs in front of entrances.
The hummingbirds visit while you are naked.
The cats do not like moles for lunch.
The mudwasp's sting will enlarge the thigh
more than a yellow jacket's.
Sweet Williams grow after tulips the best.
Plumbing will go when the north wind blows,
six weeks after the onset of frost, it will last.
Screeching owls like red sunsets.
Dogs love to watch bunnies in the garden.
Comfrey will take over, only beaten out by the blackberry forest.
It's possible to keep a soup pot going for two weeks, the same stock.
And there is nothing like running outside naked for a log, in mid
December.

Tropical night

The rain
glistening
on the women's shoulders
pleases the night.

The jungle
encroaching on the city
allows
only so much freedom.

I do not know which moment you reach out
taking my breath away,
touching all the women's breasts.

I do not know which moment you retreat
leaving us naked
as morning comes dancing.

Desire

the alarm did not go off, the morning started without that jarring noise
you floated above the ground, effortlessly, i followed your movements
hair wet and glistening about your shoulders
the taut body arching over the sink
your eyes, the sky falling into my heart
you crushed the crusty vessel
the flood of stars engulfed both of us
it happens once in a millennia, it happens.

You left for work, I stood in my room, feeling your movement
the whole body knowing your presence
never too far, never absent in my life

The nightgown hung quietly on the hook
I opened the closet door and it caught my breath
my face covered with your scent, I revealed in our life.
My life, that began with you always there
never knowing that you would materialize at 45 of my years
later than wanted but just in time
the star that you caught was falling without anchors or that pull
that makes one shine
oh, so vivid the dreams are now, so full it makes that aching sweet
you come into my life
as I gently enter yours.
5 cats and a dog, we turn our faces
I can see tomorrow, clearly

a tremor
gentling aftershock
you holding time
concentric waves
into infinity
I extend myself

About this night that goes deeply

It is Wednesday day
Kate Wolf ballads smooth the day
I recall you being stopped by her voice
In a song that called you to mind

I held you in my sight, listened to
You whispering the song, contralto
I am amazed elated and surrounded
By your scent

A memory of the night pulling
Us into each other, so wanting
So full and open, baby
You say, come here…I know

Now even
I learned you and myself
time graces us with
Never felt experiences
(Or is it just I)
Hold me tongue tied

A moment and I am into infinity
In the palm of your hand, I cry to
Ease this joy skirting
Madness of this wanting
You

Frequently, forever.

Waiting

Thursday morning the angel came
sweet mile on my lips and honey
between my legs
she sang among the water drops
the shower rang with her strength
I sat and listened, it was the morning
when the angel visited.

April 8

It is the 8th of April
the morning sun shines through the blinds
wakes the thoughts to dance
the air streams, it flows and curves up
like the feelings inside, emerge
as a dream I had
as the life I lead
so many days in between, the thirst gathers
it twists and figure eights
the waiting for words that have not escaped your pen
is long
between the letters
is long
before my thirst is quieted
is long.

I like this waiting
for your kiss
for dinner to warm up
for letters from afar
for words of encouragement
I demand nothing but wait and wait
life is waiting to happen when the moment is ripe.

Waiting is time measured in slowed breath
waiting is enough time for her fruit to open
waiting is the thought that surfaces
waiting is enough for loves and monks
waiting for the words to light the fire the fireplace cold unless
you have waited for the tree to cycle and give you wood
waiting is the essence of moments piling up for the harvest.
Do not be harsh on her. Waiting the the twin sister of doing.

Bathed in moon light
a cat, three pillows and you on the bed
you whispered in my ear
there is nothing like this

you in my arms
a full moon feeling
august evening settles in on cicada wings
your words "nothing like this" it haunts me again
I gain a new wisdom in every kiss

At Lake Williams

Pleasure sits like a stone on her tongue
Cool, smooth, centering
making her remember again
the pleasure of riding a horse
the rhythm in waking up
the joy she feels between her legs
unmoving, spiraling
yet intently focused
allowing the stone to vibrate
'til it shatters into myriads of stars.
The spring breeze shakes her hair
touching her dreams
fleetingly sprite.
She hold her stones to her breasts
naked.
She dives into the lake
releasing with each stone a dream
as they settle at the bottom
her eyes open wide, searching the murky water
for sparks of fire.
She is exploding for lack of air
and chooses to remain
rooted
among swaying grass
holds on
a moment longer
to see the face of God
then
like a shooting star
cuts through the sky
for the final intake of air
the first breath again and again.
The stones have left her tongue and her heart.
Belly down on the shore
she gasps and recalls herself.

At your therapist

Are you talking about missing your
        Family and your motherland?
Are you still warm?

Amazed

What did you tell your friends
What did they ask
Who do you want to know what?

With you soon…

        You nurture me
        Wanted to hold me, and feed me–
        Maybe
        I am a bird–no–
        Just me.

Started to breathe faster–

Amazed

With you soon

Among the differences
Finding
The thread of similarities
Amazed

A beginning this way
And time will tell

How long
      How long
We hold this sacred

The ability to go the distance
To build in rare air

Vow the future and the present shifts
With your smile and eyes embracing my soul
Is all there

Will you remember the future
Hold the present moment
A second not too late
I breathe faster
Vow my heart to myself
Opening to you

Sit still
Be quiet, oh hush
Remember the sun coming
Through naked branches, a spider web shape
Perfect
Warm water
And there you are–here.

You are difficult to your self only
Know that, and turn your good hand
To collect the bright ness I call you
And me the undeniable vessel
In this happiest moment

Amazed
Accepting
Sharing
A bulb turning into flower
      In my garden, scented
Cooking, alone but with you in there
Now you are

Energy and environment
E to the square
You multiplied by yourself
Immeasurable see too

What I can imagine, you have lived
The vision and wisdom to know yet
You remain open and now you are here
Inside the acceleration of intent
A force of your presence like
An iris in a field of poppies

already dancing.

But what can I do, I am happy when I am with you

The nightgown warms me to your scent
The telephone is silent too long
your voice is just an echo away
simmering between my legs.

The aches and pains are a welcomed guest
along my body they announce your presence in the past
The morning is too long before your call
filled with enormous cells of silence
I wait for my heart to begin the day
I wait for the bells to announce that once again
you are among my arms, content for a moment yet hungry for my eyes
each moment a present of the future to be
shall I skid away not fulfilling the want that is there everpresent
in you and me, without this world, without those stars
life could be a dull moment
but the shooting star catches my breath
brining me into the possibility that this dream shall pass
leaving us hungry and searching for the rest of our lives
for that taste that is you and me, separately yet combined.

The birds of passion
emerge from a realm
I am running from.

Where the divide
runs them aground
the shores
with oh-such
clear blue-shimmer
greet the day again.

never do I go
never do I cry
not for you
not for me
I go into chaos
I emerge clean.
The breath of
the child
bathes me new.
This day
the crows are
outside my
front window
but I do
not come
out.

August's farewell brought your arrival
the shadows branched
the moon lit up the left side of your face
where I planted the first kiss for the
rest of my life that light
will bring you to heart

you can choose to be there or not
no matter
the power of love
has taken its first breath
the hunger grows for your touch

the soft of your neck, arching like a bridge
reaching for the other shore
where I stood enchanted, lost in
that moment, reaching for your hand.

lover's blue covers my body
moments of clarity cloud my day
in lust, I find myself
and I found myself once again.

Sleep avoids my courtyard
Each moment has a new sound
to be held, to be caressed
I feel again, myself

Love comes shamelessly
Love comes without punishment
Love comes to cure the heart
Love comes to embrace us in compassion

Lovers have no quarrels, true love
makes the moss green, gentling
our passages, our paths
Love never ends, will you turn towards me?

The color blue has inviting eyes
the waves wash over me
emerging and diving for purple memories
It was yesterday, not before that
I recognized her smile
The tentative look, yes come hither child,

The giants roam no more, motherless we are
The herons fly from memory
The turtles with ancient houses
It is the friday morning that we all
immersed in blue
It is the morning
we give our voices to each other.

Deep where the stars fall

Deep where the stars fall
there is no resistance.

The light is everlasting
the knowing, endless.

It is there that I stood in front of you,
naked to the soul, but you resisted.

I held my breath
and prayed for your awakening.

I looked to the right, then left.

I swallowed myself
in order to know the truth.

each pebble is the essence of life
slowly
         time engraves its marks
but who looks at the pebble
                  not i or you
it is me you are not looking at
it is me being marked by time

a child takes such delight in each pebble
              do you or do i?

the silence of the pebble is what you hear not
or listen to not
each wave or wind brush creates or destroys
have we got the time
and you ask me how and why i love you
and what i see in you
all, my dear
the summation of each and all pebbles that we
are or are not
i see you smile and see not the pebble
why the time goes and you are not within
and all the pebbles
              that are you and me
and you ask me why i love you.

Early love poem   11/20/1993

The warmth
the legs apart yet holding you within
the shack by the road
a blanket that is like velvet
your lips smooth and urging
your hands strong and encouraging
music of butterflies
breathing in breathing out.

Where shadows cling to memories
where the ivy tunnels the direction
where the sun evades your smile
where the view entangled in your hair
the curve of your mouth
drives me mad to be without.

Your nipples like mountains take my breath away
Your secrets behind your ears take my breath away
Your breathless rhythm takes my breath away
Your heavenly cry only a breath away

Desire

Curving, pulling me in-
side myself, the pulse
plays the song that thickens my blood.
Where do I call you,
Reason for madness,
your thighs softly evading
my desires
how long, how long
before you crave my flesh
how long, how long
before your return to the well
the web, your own trap
you have already woven
why evade
the bones and the flesh
the veins like twine twist and shriek
after you sucked me
clean, oh so clean.

Hotel Europa

The night fell on Quito
as I fell on your lips.
The warmth of your neck
where it is softest, lingers.

The lips polishing the diamond
and yet not hard.

The fingers opening petals
yet the world is closing.

The tongue searching the mouth
yet aching for the soul.

Goddesses Atticus

wet
you mix colors of light
your arms fly and smooth your

nipples
the hands roll and turn the world
the hair floats in my mind
under my breasts
under my lower back
i imagine you
smiling
in bed at night
the angel by your side

green velvet
mineral water with ice
a slice of lime
cool lips
the moon sits on your side of the bed
invites all that it brings
in moonlight velvet i sing.

Emerald body

your nipples arched to meet my lips
a wetness rushing
clouds gather touching the souls of my feet
the flow curves and bends on itself
the space under my breast echoes
your hand on me demands heat
the music strikes your darkness
sparks on the deepened green moss
your lips cooled by ice touching
the folds dive for pearls to be born
diamonds fall from your eyelashes
emerald bodied. I lose my senses.

To the one I love

you came, visited the sick and the well
the morning lifted your footsteps off cement sidewalks
it reeled the stars around as they hit
the ground red and the black sky never faded
you looked so young and happy through my eyes
the whore of the town was envious of your thighs
the shadow ached for your touch
i sang your name
the milk flowed with honey on my lips
and the music screamed its melody through my iris
it never expect to arrive
the walls allowed your echo to permeate
to balance the desire in my mind.

the air whirls around the skirt you wear
you sing hymns in restaurants
the women in pearls wince at your sight
i recline in the chair and smile at you
the miracle you replace in my world is
the miracle i needed in my life.

the years come to fourteen at the turn of the clock
where have we been?

my mother told me the sin of her life
i wept and forgave her for letting down her guard
you came and saw my pain
you suffered leonard's songs
you lead me to the beach and made me look
at broken seashells, the colors
the sharp edges that you fingered with your splendid tongue.
i ache for you and the sweat that covered your body at my touch.

Lover

Like the fox
speeding softly in the snow
leaving tracks of flight from the cold
I come to warm you.
I come to teach your
beating heart
that
I care for you.
Fingers
arching backs
I take you to myself
and for one lifetime
I will show you
how we are of each.
The sun warms our naked shadows
reflecting on them
shadows as light and soft
as that of the running fox.

Lips parted
your body eased its
way onto mine.
The cat settled by our tangled feet
in the rhythm of shadows, in flickering light.

Lips parted
your thighs urging between mine,
shifting the weight
left to right
The ocean,
the tides
rushing.

Lips parted
shyness
left to right
urging
tides rushing
all is left behind
your shyness electrified our journey.

Declaration

She ate words
She ached in familiar places
love lifted chaos
She pounded her heart and sang

for thirtythree years now
She ate words three thousand times a day
avoiding only one from consumption
holding it in her palm
resonating in her bones:
She is a lesbian

She says it faintly first
I am a lesbian
then
like the train's approach
the words roar through her hair
I am
I was
I will always be
Divinely yours, a lesbian.

at sundown
i reached for you
LOOK, THE SUN
for the first time
and
        last
i saw the red sky
like the sea
swallow the red ball
glowing

Afterthought

The lightning

reaches across the sky.

The air fills

with moments

that have been electrified.

The words

run out just before

you see the face of god in lovemaking.

Grief

do not turn around do not turn around
the voice kept repeating in my mind
do not look to yesterday, yesterday
it is all in the tomorrows

you make your fate your sorrow
you burn the candles out, with it
burns your soul, do not turn around
the somewheres of your mind remind you of
everything that touched you and nothing
that's new or old will go unnoticed or
will it with it your life unnoticed.
only do not turn around, turn around
make your choice of yes or no
let the shadows glide from the past as
the sunshine for the future, do not
turn around, do not turn around.

if it be that simple, of not turning
ever looking back, that's all
life would be a playground and we all
remain within the children
let the wind under your wings show
the birds you can soar just as high
be the bird of life do not turn around.

dreams mingling with my days
images of mother and sister
bombed house shells, no roofs
all are within my vision of life

many men have passed the night
echolessly   shadows are softer
no images in the mirror
end of the summer is end of my life.

EVA

you are dead, sixty four days, now
have
        i been without you

six feet under the ground
dearest
six feet under the ground
and i go on living
six feet   above the ground
dearest
six feet above the ground
what can I tell you
people still trample on each other
wars have not stopped their raging
all has remained the same or worse
and i listen to music and feel ill
and i listen to you too and cry
since i am not sure if you can hear it
can you
six feet under the ground
dearest
six feet under the ground.

no dreams
no feelings
no echoes
the heart is invisible and without shadow
the reminders are many and solid
you are not here and
I know not the land you roam
or your heart
where is your echo
the shadows remain hidden
the songs are distant
turning the ring you gave me
the bracelet broke
signs are foreboding
the signs are there though
come alive
come back
I await your return.

desires died yesterday
the snow fell at the silent speed
at the crack of dawn i asked for you
the head was turned the other way
wind awake later in the day
dried my tears on my face
gray marks of happiness engraved.

i do not know what will make me happy anymore
yesteryear was such a long ago
the moon was ever so bright
the music flow was easy in my heart
stormy waves of emotion blind me in my search
I do not see the road or feel the way
the winds blows
cliches come back
over and over again
like a disease spreads and contaminates the air
birth and freedom and wordflow
i await patiently for your coming age
this is the time for your arrival
there is a reason to wait

silence has begun
disturbing thoughts are gone
where to- - -deeper where I cannot reach
silence has begun.

come, let me show you my place
she said, come for tea
I have been doing stone work

I turn my head and avoid heart pain
it is said with such ease
the memories flood me with sadness
of times before when she could think of
nothing but leave and busy ourselves with
outside events, the distractions
like a knife cut into my heart but I
went because I wanted to be with her
and happiness still avoided our hearts

is that true, was that so bad?
I ask now and there is no answer,
not even
an echo that tells yes,
it was real

fourteen years, does that mean any thing to you
my heart screams into my own void
she is not there, not even in the void to answer
because she chooses not to be attached

so helpless my heart flops around
not finding a point, the common ground of our past
a place even to stand on and start over again

but without you, I tell the wind
but without you.

August 18, 1993

hot humid moments fly like mallards for cooler climate
I hang from the beaks scraping the sky so low
the meadows touch my heels
I scream from pain inside
the yellow in the sun escapes me
the yes of Horus blink
its knowledge beckons to me
bow your head
open your hearts
the grass is even growing for your footsteps
the drumming echoes in my cells
come to me…come to me, over and over again
the heart give its echoes to the moon
the shallow lake begs for forgiveness
the pebbles imprint your dna
yellow yellow
feeling empty,
is half full, there is more to give and more to receive
is is like the songs un sung
the memories give it its shape
the notes skip on the high wire as my head glides toward you
to clutch the emptiness you left behind
but the heart keeps whispering the unknown
who will translate for me now.

Crescent Moon
starry skies
crows are singing
I have no smile

Sky heavy
pregnant with gray
future snow flakes
of crystal rain
that may fall
today
as our lives
heavy with our
future May
as our lives
gray, pregnant
with pain
it will never mend
sky opening with
thunderous pain

Thin white blanket
is covering
our minds
so afraid
of the slippery
ice
we just stare
with cloudy
eyes

White and gray
the seashore line
the water mixed
with sound
with waves
start and strong
winter spell
the birds
of

white walls
are cold
same as the sky
gray and white
today
Sun out.

changing the day
night sneaked up through this rainbow
changing-pain
cuts down my shoulder, shaking
come alive-change
       green to blue
i sneak across your room
tears do not flow down my cheeks
following the sun
we become one-in-all, in one.

Calling on Angels

The skit is full of sadness
It is the twentyfirst of November
my father, in a hospital bed
both legs amputated, the disease at them
chaos like a windstorm makes his way around
winter sighs
allowing the flow of energy to emulate life

I yearn for peace and painless passage for him
I call forth the spring of his youth
the tenacity of his thirties
to help him bridge this river
we call life to ashes

I call my father a man of qualities and his are many,
among them integrity, honesty, forthrightness and
commitment, none of these are lacking in him
I call on God to help him
shed his burden, ease his pain and ours

I call on my mother to keep her heart and love
for him intact as she has done for fortynine years and more
I call on my brother to realize the minute scrimmages
fathers and sons have,
these none call a gap

I call on my sister to heal her pain
and forgive the trespasses
intent with honesty and protection at best
all is well in a healed and forgiving heart
Can he forgive us and himself

We have all done our best
worked for each penny with honest sweat
we called a tulip by its name
a flower as it opened, we closed our eyes
closed a chapter in history, his and ours

Calling on angels, calling on angels
a great man is approaching
calling on angels, calling on angels

The candle melted in the shape of
Wings, two around the stem in lavender wax
Like the wings mother needed to
Fly to heaven. She had them

As she breathed out, and not in
Ever again.
It was a Tuesday noon, all gathered around her
We tended and honored her life, her children.

How delicate, fragile is the lifeline
We take for granted, every day

The moment we realized she is
Not coming back, we prayed and
Sang for her journey, eyes wet
And broken hearts for the lack
Of what we did not know yet at that moment

She would be with us
Stronger and more in every moment
As we progress our days and nights

How immeasurable the loss is of
One's mother, I can only express
With strength and joy for them life given
Into this body and the other two children.

The Bible, and the Tibetan Book of living and the dying
Were read and her favorite hymns sang
All to ease us into life again
Fatherless and motherless
We stand, like a gang of outcasts on the street corners

We will be our parent's children now
More than ever before.
We stood and sat around her body for
Seven hours more before we could let her
Go to ashes.

The men came, all in black
Covered her face and I begged for them not to do that
Wheeled her out through the kitchen and
Down the walkway to a van, unmarked
As the stars gathered above us, bright.

Ydune

You left early this earthly path.
....
....

I greet each day for you and me.
....
....

I dance on earth, you dance in heaven.
....
....

The gates to my soul opened
....
....

You are on the right
....
....

Father on the left
....
....

Grandmothers looking over
....
....

Grandfathers singing
....
....

....
....

What is that…but heaven.

Blue Hour

At times like this
time is light yellow, you notice
at that time
time is as coal dust.

The house sits defined
breathing in daytime
exhaling into the milky way
immeasurably.

We shudder in bed each 4 am
the time tides shift back
the time the sounds lift soundless
between light and darkness
above the houses, closing in on heaven
yet chimneystruck, lingering
untangling their webs in such silence.
Their echoes
rattling the figurines on the mantelpiece.

All falls silent as the first light molecule
turns to face our planet,
momentarily yet eternally
each timescape forms the landscape
sudden, bereft, seemingly joyful.

It was a clear night, a hold night.
We gave her over to God, into heaven
To join her parents, husband and granddaughter
We were left lacking yet full of her in our life already.

A stiff drink was called for, we toasted her journey and
Kept drinking to ease our fear of what next.
Gail friend stood by us and held whomever needed
To be held, the strength and grounding needed.

Two days before she left, we were making plans for
Thanksgiving dinner and her moving
upstairs to her own bed, when she got well.

The acupuncturist said,
Now play music and read poetry to her,
like the love poem she was in our lives
She knew the change has happened before
We knew it not and could not believe it.

The nurse was there from hospice for the night
Like the angel of death, hovering around us
Her silence and intermittent questions
Interrupting at times, yet felt right
To have an experienced soul around.

I recall the air around my face, smooth and different
I recall the dusk falling around us
I recall the tears flowing down my face
The grip of hands, my sister and brother
That kept me upright.

I want her back, no doubt, hands down, ready
To take her for my lifetime.
I want her at peace and joy
Among the clouds, smiling
Down on us, her moment of joy with father.

How to do my best now is a requirement
In memory and in life
An honoring of their lives too
in honor of mine
Let go, they say, let go
Be merry, eat, drink and celebrate
Breath in, breath out
staying alive.

Eden, Paradiso, Menyország

Sun flowers in sun shine
sun stricken blind life
sun centered mythos cries
me the flower, you see it?

sun folded smile
sending power to twilight
Thy will is done

you and I hold the memories
sun flower shine of Ydune
in Eden, Paradiso, Menyország.

What do I know?

What I know is
that I know little about what another death
will mean to me.
Will you fall asleep
while we are holding hands,
palm to palm
lips afraid of the separation?
Will I stop counting sheep?
The pressure on my belly will it get heavier, deeper?
The curve of your back up against the line where hair meets the softness.
What do I know of this moment and the void that will follow forever?

About the Author

Emőke B'Rácz is a poet, artist, and founder of Malaprop's Bookstore/Cafe and Downtown Books & News. She was voted Best Bookseller in the US by Publishers Weekly. Her previous books include *Hungarian Refugee* and *Remember Me as a Time of Day*. Emőke is the founder of Burning Bush Asheville and One Page Press, and was awarded an inclusion in the Women Making History by the ACT. She has been published in Nexus, Visions, Woman Words, Webster Review, Asheville Poetry Review, Hungarian Review, New Native Press, and New York Quarterly and has translated the works of Katalin Ladik, Zoltán Zelk, and Ilyes Gyula. Emőke lives in Asheville, North Carolina.

www.ingramcontent.com/pod-product-compliance
Lightning Source LLC
Chambersburg PA
CBHW032036290426
44110CB00012B/820